The REFORMED And PRESBYTERIAN FAITH

A View from Nigeria

Rev. Timothy Palmer, Ph.D.

TCNN PUBLICATIONS
Bukuru, Plateau State, Nigeria

**The Reformed and Presbyterian Faith:
A View from Nigeria**

Copyright © 1996 Timothy Palmer

ISBN 978-2668-63-X
CAPRO Media, Box 6001, Jos, Nigeria

First Print, Feb.,1996 - 4,000 copies

All rights reserved. This publication is copyright protected. No part of this publication may be reproduced, stored in a retrieval system, transmitted, or reproduced in any way, including but not limited to photocopy, photograph, magnetic or record, without the prior agreement and written permission of the publisher.

TCNN PUBLICATIONS
Theological College of Northern Nigeria
P. O. Box 64, Bukuru, Plateau State, Nigeria

Distributed in Nigeria and West Africa by
African Christian TextbookS (ACTS)
P. O. Box 64, Bukuru, Plateau State, Nigeria.

Order from
The Bookshop, TCNN
P. O. Box 64, Bukuru, Plateau State, Nigeria.

Produced in the Federal Republic of Nigeria
by CAPRO Media Services, P.O Box 6001, Jos.

Table of Contents

Preface   1

PART I. REFORMED AND PRESBYTERIAN HISTORY   3

1. Historical Background   3
    The Church as a Tree   3
    Ulrich Zwingli   7

2. John Calvin   9

3. Scotland and England   16
    Scotland   16
    England   20

4. France, Germany and Eastern Europe   24
    France   24
    Germany   26
    Eastern Europe   27

5. The Netherlands   29
    The Dutch Reformation   29
    The Synod of Dort   30
    The (Dutch) Christian Reformed Church   33
    Netherlands Reformed Congregations   35

6. **North America and South Africa**	**37**
North America	37
South Africa	40
7. **Southern Nigeria**	**43**
Presbyterian Church of Nigeria	43
Qua Iboe Church	47
Nigeria Reformed Church	50
8. **Northern Nigeria**	**52**
Christian Reformed Church in Nigeria	54
Reformed Church of Christ in Nigeria	57
Nongo u Kristu u ken Sudan hen Tiv	59
Evangelical Reformed Church of Christ	63
9. **Reformed Ecumenical Fellowships**	**66**
World Alliance of Reformed Churches	67
Reformed Ecumenical Council	67
Reformed Ecumencial Council of Nigeria	68
PART II. REFORMED AND PRESBYTERIAN BELIEFS	**70**
10. **The Reformed Worldview: The Lordship of God**	**70**
The Reformed Worldview	72
The Kingdom of God	74
The King of the Kingdom	76
The Scepter of the King: Scripture	78

11.	**God's Lordship in Conversion: Election**	**81**
	Election	81
	Irresistible Grace	85
	Total Depravity	86
	Perseverance of the Saints	87
	Limited Atonement	88
	Five Points of Calvinism	90
12.	**God's Lordship in History: Providence**	**92**
13.	**God's Lordship in the Christian Life: Sanctification**	**96**
	Individual Sanctification	96
	Lordship of God in Society	99
	The Law of God	102
14.	**God's Lordship in the Church**	**105**
	Church Government	107
	Baptism and the Lord's Supper	111
15.	**God's Lordship in the Future**	**116**
	The Millenium	118

Conclusion   123

Bibliography   124

Map of Europe in 1500

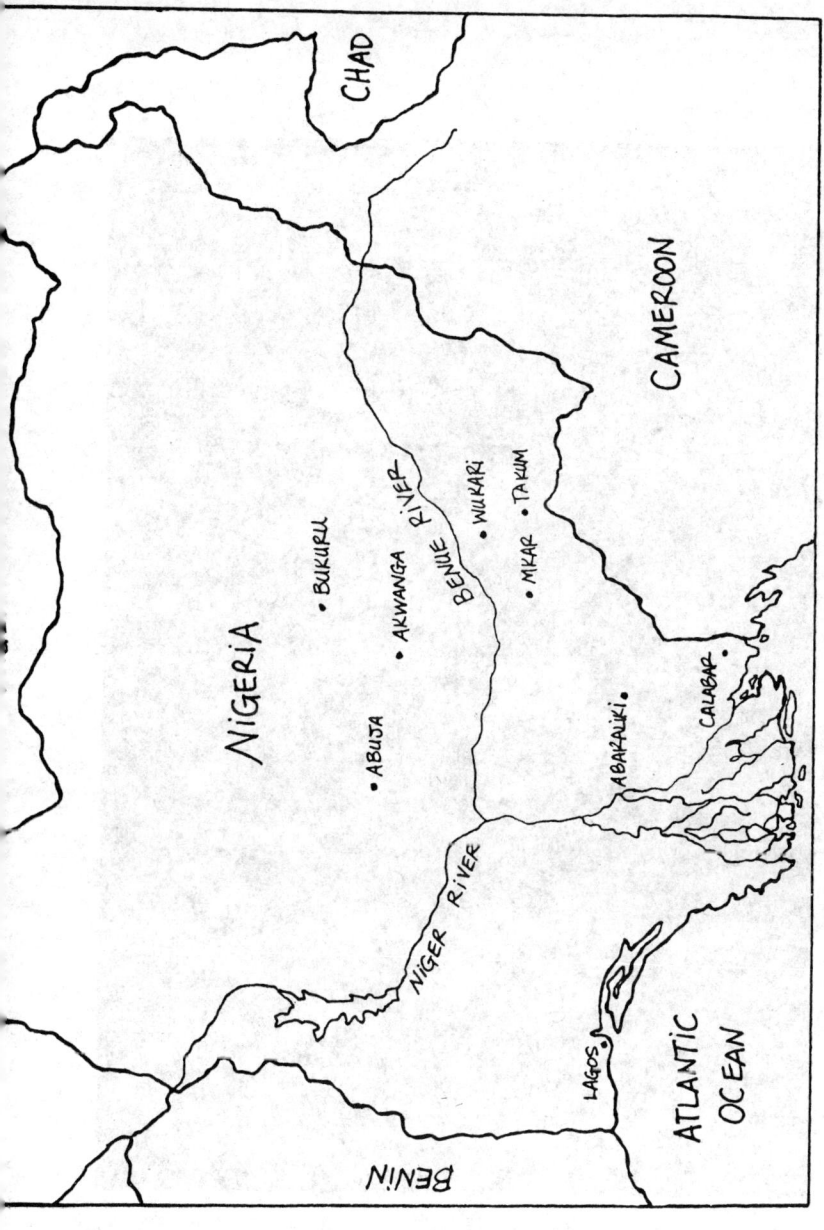

Map of Nigeria

John Calvin

Preface

Many Christians in Nigeria belong to churches that have the name Reformed or Presbyterian. We have the Presbyterian Church of Nigeria (PCN), the Evangelical Reformed Church of Christ (ERCC), the Christian Reformed Church of Nigeria (CRCN), the Reformed Church of Christ in Nigeria (RCCN) and the Nigeria Reformed Church (NRC). There are also churches like the Nongo u Kristu u ken Sudan hen Tiv (NKST) and the Qua Iboe Church, which are Reformed in their theology.

But many of us do not know what it means to be Reformed or Presbyterian. We call ourselves by these names, but we don't always know the meaning of these names. This book is written to help us understand who we are. It is also written to help other Christians understand the Reformed faith.

This book has two parts. The first part is historical. It traces the history of the Reformed movement from its origins to Nigeria. In this section you can discover the roots of your own church. Where did your church come from? Who are you really?

The second part summarizes the main beliefs of the Reformed and Presbyterian churches. Here you can find something about the special teachings of your church. What do we believe? How do our churches differ from other churches?

This book can be read selectively. You may wish to read the historical chapters that are relevant to your own church. You may also concentrate on the doctrinal, or second, part. But the chapter on John Calvin should be read by all since he is the founder of the Reformed movement.

I want to thank the Reformed and Presbyterian students at the Theological College of Northern Nigeria (TCNN), Bukuru, who urged me to write this book. Many of these issues were discussed in our denominational class.

I also want to thank all of the people who read the manuscript in its draft form. My thanks goes especially to Kim Fynewever for the illustration of the tree and the maps, and also to John Bakker for his advice on the cover.

The publication of this book coincides with the 150th anniversary of the coming of the Gospel to the Presbyterian area of Nigeria. In 1846 Rev. Hope Waddell and his party arrived in Calabar. It is my hope that this book will help the Presbyterians in their celebration of this event. But I pray that this book will be used by each Reformed church to stimulate a greater awareness of its identity.

Theological College of Northern Nigeria
Bukuru
January 1, 1996

PART ONE.

REFORMED AND PRESBYTERIAN HISTORY

Chapter One

Historical Background

The church of Jesus Christ is one. The apostle Paul says that "there is one body and one Spirit, ... one Lord, one faith, one baptism" (Eph. 4:4-5). As long as we confess the name of Jesus, we are part of the one body of Christ.

However, in this church there are different branches. These branches have developed because of cultural, geographic, linguistic, historical or doctrinal reasons. There are Baptist, Lutheran, Methodist and Reformed churches. There are both Nigerian and Scottish Presbyterian churches. There are Dutch and Tiv Reformed churches.

In order to understand who we are, we have to know something about our history. Where do we come from? How did our church begin?

The Church as a Tree

The church can be compared to a tree with many branches. The Apostle Paul in the Book of Romans compared the church of Christ to an olive tree with different branches (Rom. 11:11-24). The trunk of the tree is Israel. The Jewish branches that did not believe were cut off. Gentile Christians who believed in Jesus were grafted into this tree. This tree with these new branches is now the new Israel. The church through its history has many branches. There are Catholic, Lutheran, Baptist and Methodist branches, as well as Reformed and Presbyterian ones, to name just a few.

The root of this great tree is Jesus Christ. When Jesus asked his disciples who people thought he was, he received many answers. Some thought he was John the Baptist, others Elijah, and others one of the prophets. But when Jesus asked them who they thought he was, Peter said: "You are the Christ [Messiah], the Son of the living God." Jesus replied that on the rock of this confession he would build his church (Matt. 16:13-18). Thus the foundation or root of the universal church is Jesus Christ and the confession that he is the Messiah, the Son of God.

In his first letter, Peter compares the church to a temple built of stones. He says that the cornerstone of the building is Jesus (1 Peter 2:4-8.) So Jesus is both the foundation and the root of the tree.

The trunk of the tree comes out of this root. In the first five hundred years of the church's history, the church in the Roman Empire was basically one. We can picture this early church as the trunk of the tree.

Although it was one, this church spoke two languages. In the East it spoke Greek; in the West it spoke Latin. Gradually the Eastern and Western churches drifted apart. The Eastern church is usually called the Greek Orthodox Church; today it has national branches like the Russian Orthodox Church. The Western church became the Roman Catholic Church. The division between the Eastern and Western branches was finalized in 1054.

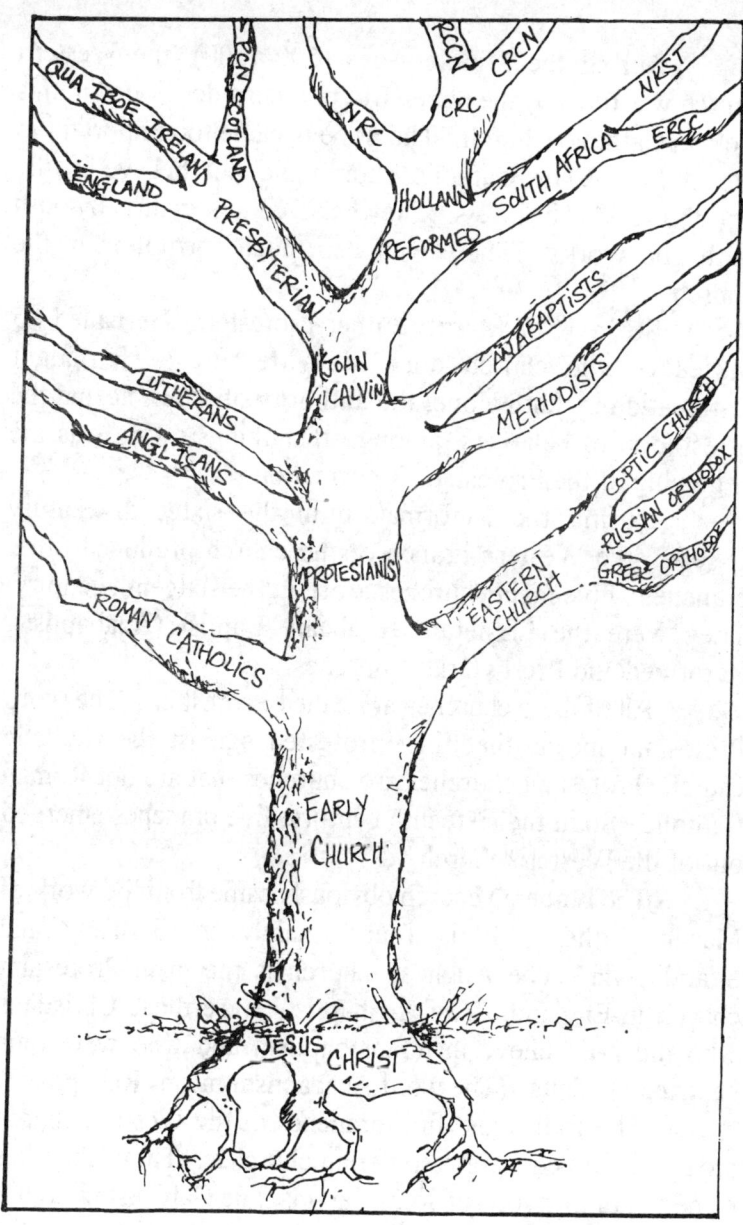

The Church Pictured as a Tree

During the Middle Ages (500-1500), the Western church was ruled by the pope. But problems developed in this Roman Catholic Church. The pope became too important in the church. The Catholic church did not believe in the priesthood of all believers. They believed in salvation by both faith and works. There was also much corruption in the church.

So in 1517 Martin Luther protested. He nailed 95 theses on the church door in Wittenberg. He taught justification by faith alone, the authority of the Bible and the priesthood of believers, among other things. This was the beginning of the Protestant Reformation.

During the Reformation in the sixteenth century (1500s), the Western branch of the church produced other branches. Five main churches arose in the sixteenth century. They were the Lutheran, Anglican, Baptist (Anabaptist), Reformed and Presbyterian churches.

All of these churches are called Protestant. The word Protestant means that they protested against the Catholic church. Protestant churches are churches that are not Roman Catholic. So in the sixteenth century, five branches emerged out of the Western church.

The Lutheran church obviously came from the work of Martin Luther. It is found mainly in Germany and Scandinavia. The Anglican church is the main Protestant church in England. The Anabaptists were those Christians who did not believe in infant baptism and who were thus baptized as adults. (The word Anabaptism means Rebaptism.)

The fourth and fifth branches of the Western church are the Reformed and Presbyterian churches. These churches came out of the work of John Calvin. The Calvinist churches in England and Scotland were called Presbyterian; the Calvinist churches in the rest of Europe were called Reformed.

You can see that ethnic or tribal factors were important in the formation of European Protestant churches. German Protestants were usually Lutheran; Scottish Protestants were Presbyterian, Dutch Protestants were Reformed; English Protestants were either Presbyterian or Anglican.

Ulrich Zwingli

The origins of the Reformed and Presbyterian churches are found in the country of Switzerland. Switzerland is a small mountainous country in the center of Europe. An important city in Switzerland is Zurich. On January 1, 1519, the big Catholic church in Zurich received a new pastor. His name was Ulrich Zwingli (1484-1531). Zwingli knew the Greek language, and he had memorized all of Paul's writings in Greek! The Bible was very important for him.
    Zwingli began his ministry in Zurich by preaching through the whole Gospel of Matthew, chapter by chapter and verse by verse. Many of the people in his church and in the city realized the power of the Word of God for the first time. Within a few years the Reformed church was established in Zurich. The doctrine of Scripture as the Word of God has always been a central part of the Reformed faith.   Zwingli came from the German-speaking part of Switzerland. He laid the foundation for the Reformed church. However the true "father" of the Reformed church worked in the French-speaking part of Switzerland. His name was John Calvin.

Study Questions

1. What is the root or foundation of the church?
2. What is the original trunk of the church?

3. What are the first two main branches of the church? Why did they develop?
4. Why did the Western branch of the church sprout other branches?
5. What does the word "Protestant" mean?
6. Describe the ethnic nature of the five sixteenth-century Protestant churches.
7. What is the difference between "Reformed" and "Presbyterian"?
8. What was the main principle of the Reformed church in Zurich?

Chapter Two

John Calvin

John Calvin was born in the north of France, in the city of Noyon. He was born on July 10, 1509, eight years before Luther started the Reformation. Calvin was thus born in the Catholic church. He studied law at a few French universities, and he received his degree in law.

While studying at the university, Calvin, like Zwingli, came under the influence of the Renaissance. So Calvin learned Greek and Hebrew in order to read the Bible in the original languages.

During his days as a student, Calvin came into contact with the ideas of Luther. Calvin and his friends discussed some of these ideas and were sympathetic to them. At this time you could call Calvin a Lutheran!

On November 1, 1533, a friend of Calvin, Nicholas Cop, gave a speech at the University of Paris advocating Lutheran sentiments. Calvin and Cop then had to flee from Paris because of possible persecution. In October 1534, anti-Catholic posters were displayed in Paris, so the situation remained dangerous for him. In early 1535 he fled from France to the city of Basel in Switzerland.

In the Preface to Calvin's Commentary on the Psalms we have a beautiful and important autobiographical sketch of Calvin. In these pages we read how God led Calvin by his providence to serve him and his church. In this preface Calvin mentions his "sudden conversion," presumably the time when he broke with the Roman Catholic church and became Protestant. This probably occurred in 1533 or 1534.

By 1535 the French king was persecuting the Protestants. Many Catholics did not fully understand the Protestant faith. In the quiet safety of Basel, Calvin decided to write a book clearly explaining the Protestant faith. This work, published in 1536, is the first edition of the *Institutes of the Christian Religion*. It is a clear and systematic presentation of the Christian faith. The book has an impassioned prefatory letter written to King Francis I defending the French Protestants. In this work Calvin put himself forward as a leader of the Protestant movement. Calvin was only 26 years old when he wrote this book.

The 1536 edition of the *Institutes* is based on Luther's Catechism. The first four chapters are an explanation of the Ten Commandments, the Apostles' Creed, the Lord's Prayer and the two sacraments. The last two chapters are against Catholic teachings on the sacraments and the government. In the next twenty years Calvin revised and expanded the *Institutes* many times until by 1559 it reached its final and much larger form.

After spending about a year in Basel, Calvin traveled through France, but it was still not safe for him. In July 1536 when he was passing through Switzerland again, he came to the city of Geneva, intending to leave the next morning. But the pastor of Geneva, a fiery preacher by the name of William Farel, heard that Calvin was in town. He found him and asked him to stay in Geneva to help pastor the church there. Calvin protested saying that he would like to go to a quiet place and continue an academic life. But Farel said that God would judge him if he did not stay in Geneva. In this way Calvin received a strong call to serve God in Geneva. (You can read Calvin's account of this encounter in the Preface to his Commentary on the Psalms.)

Geneva had only recently become Protestant. On May 21, 1536, all the citizens of Geneva had come into the marketplace and had sworn with uplifted hands to live by the Word of God and to abandon idolatry. In other words, they had decided to forsake the Roman Catholic religion and had chosen the Protestant faith. Geneva was then a city with about 10,000 people that needed strong pastoral leadership. Thus Farel, who was an older man, felt that he needed the help of Calvin, who was only 27 years old and who had proved himself to be a convinced Protestant.

From the start Calvin affirmed the lordship of God. He believed that God should be Lord and King over our lives. He taught that all of life is to be subject to the kingship of Christ. This belief meant that for him sanctification was very important. It is not enough to confess Jesus as one's Savior; one must also apply this lordship of Christ to one's life. Therefore church discipline was an important way of keeping believers faithful to God in their daily lives. However Calvin ran into a disagreement with the city government about church discipline. The issue was: who should administer church discipline, the city government or the church council? Both sides claimed the right for themselves. Because Calvin and Farel refused to yield on this issue, they were banished from Geneva on April 23, 1538, after Calvin had spent only two years in the city. Their work in Geneva seemed to have been a failure.

Calvin went to Strassburg, which was a German-speaking Protestant town. There he pastored a French-speaking congregation for three years. These three years were a quiet time for him when he was able to gain some valuable pastoral experience. He also did some writing there. He revised and expanded his *Institutes* in 1539, and he made a French translation in 1540. He wrote his first Bible commentary, on Romans, in 1539. In 1540 he married Idelette de Bure. His time in Strassburg was a peaceful time of spiritual and personal growth.

Back in Geneva things were not going well. Politically the city was in confusion, and spiritually the church was in decline. So in 1541 Calvin was officially called back to Geneva by the city council. Calvin was reluctant to jump back into the fire, but he again heard a call to serve and he returned on September 13, 1541. Before he went back he secured an agreement from the city that the church would have full authority in all church matters. He believed that the sphere of the church is separate from the sphere of the state, although of course they would interact in day-to-day affairs.

When he came to Geneva, Calvin wrote the *Ecclesiastical Ordinances*, which deals with the organization of the church. The city council adopted this document which guaranteed the freedom of the church from the state government. The ministers are "to wield only the spiritual sword of the Word of God" while the city government is to exercise only political power.

The *Ordinances* also set forth the four offices of the Reformed Church in Geneva: the offices of pastor, teacher (of the Word), elder and deacon. The pastors were to proclaim the Word of God and to administer the sacraments, in addition to their other responsibilities. The teachers or doctors of theology were to train future pastors. The elders were laymen, and they together with the pastors formed the Consistory, which was responsible for governing the church and dealing with cases of discipline. (At first there were twelve elders and six pastors in Geneva, but later the number of pastors increased. There was one Consistory for all of the churches in Geneva.) The deacons had the tasks of receiving and dispensing the church money and caring for the poor and the sick. The deacons administered a hospital in Geneva that cared for the sick and the poor.

Although Calvin wanted the Lord's Supper to be celebrated once a month in Geneva, he eventually agreed with the view of the city government; so the *Ordinances* calls for the celebration of the Lord's Supper four times a year.

Calvin remained a pastor in Geneva from 1541 until his death in 1564. Because of his conviction that Jesus Christ is to be Lord over all of our life, he attempted to make Geneva into a Christian city. Calvinism has always taken its social responsibility seriously. The Reformed churches have usually been activistic, believing that the Christian can and should transform society. Calvinism does not agree in running away from the world; instead it calls for transformation of the world.

The main criticism of Calvin on this point is that he assumed that everyone in the city of Geneva was part of the Reformed church. Thus when Michael Servetus, who denied the Trinity, came into the city, he was tried for heresy and put to death. This was decided by the city council, although it had the approval of Calvin.

Today we believe that there should be freedom of worship in our countries: a person should have the freedom to choose his own faith, and people of different religions should live peacefully with their neighbors. This is one insight that the Anabaptists already had in the sixteenth century, but which the Catholic and other Protestant churches did not accept at that time.

The little city of Geneva under the influence of Calvin soon became an important theological and ecclesiastical center. After 1534 there was systematic persecution of the Protestants in France. Many French Christians immigrated to Geneva, almost doubling the size of the city. Persecuted Christians from England and Scotland also came to Geneva for safety and to learn about the teachings of Calvin.

In 1559 the Genevan Academy was founded, which was a center of Reformed theology. The Academy was both a secondary school and a theological school which trained pastors. Many international students who were trained at this school returned to their own countries to serve as pastors. Geneva was especially important in training pastors for the Reformed church in France which was under persecution, but it also trained people from other places.

Calvin's international influence was great. His books were used throughout Europe. The *Institutes* was probably the most systematic presentation of the Protestant faith at that time. Calvin wrote commentaries on almost every book of the Bible, and these commentaries were used by Christians throughout Europe. Through the Academy, leaders of many countries were trained under Calvin's influence. In addition, Calvin corresponded with political leaders of different nations, such as King Edward VI and Queen Elizabeth I of England and the kings of Poland and Navarre. He encouraged these rulers to establish the Reformation in their kingdoms. He also wrote to important Protestant leaders to encourage them and to give them advice.

In February of 1564 Calvin had become quite ill. He was no longer able to preach or lecture. For many years he had suffered from painful illnesses, but he now had to stop his work, although he continued to meet with people in his house. Before his death he wrote to William Farel, the first reformer of Geneva, and said: "It is enough that I live and die for Christ, who is to all his followers a gain both in life and in death." Calvin died on May 27, 1564, before his 55th birthday. A great Christian had passed from this world to be with Jesus.

Calvin's successor in Geneva was Theodore Beza (1519-1605). At Calvin's death Beza became the moderator of the clergy until 1580. He was also rector of the Academy for four years before Calvin's death, and he was professor of theology for forty years (1559-1599).

Beza had a great influence in preserving and developing Calvin's theology. Although Beza taught the theology of Calvin, he had some different emphases in his theology. For example, he put a greater emphasis on predestination, putting election and reprobation at the start of his theology. (Calvin discussed election only at the end of the third book of the 1559 *Institutes*.) However, one should not overemphasize the differences between Beza and Calvin. Beza continued in Calvin's tradition, holding to the essential beliefs of his teacher.

Throughout the seventeenth century, after the death of Beza, Geneva continued to be an important center for the Reformed faith. The Academy of Geneva had become a famous institution of Protestant learning in Europe and an influential center for the Calvinist faith.

Study Questions

1. Describe how Martin Luther influenced John Calvin.
2. When and why did Calvin come to Switzerland?
3. When and why did Calvin have to leave Geneva?
4. What are the important writings of Calvin?
5. What is the most important teaching of Calvin?
6. Who are William Farel and Theodore Beza?

Chapter Three

Presbyterianism in Scotland and England

We have seen that Calvin's influence spread to many different countries. In this chapter we will look at the Reformed movement in England and Scotland. These two countries are now part of Great Britain, but in the time of Calvin they were separate nations.

Scotland

The country of Scotland is very important as the birthplace of the Presbyterian church. The origins of the Presbyterian Church of Nigeria are closely tied to the Scottish church.
    Scotland is a small hilly country north of England. In the sixteenth century it was a separate country, even though it was English-speaking.
    The king of Scotland at the time of Calvin was King James V, who ruled from 1513 to 1542. The king and his wife, Mary of Lorraine, were firmly Catholic. However, during his reign Protestantism began to penetrate the country.
    Patrick Hamilton, for example, was a young man who had gone to Germany and had discovered Luther's teachings. When he returned to Scotland he openly preached these Protestant ideas. In 1528 this man was burned at the stake by Cardinal Beaton. In 1546 the Cardinal put to death another Protestant preacher by the name of George Wishart.

George Wishart had a friend called John Knox. Knox was angry at what the Cardinal did to these Christians. Two months after Wishart was put to death, John Knox took part in a plot that put the Cardinal to death.

Young John Knox had taken a stand for the Protestant faith. But he and his companions paid for their stance. For 19 months, he and his friends were galley slaves in a French ship, chained, and forced to row for their masters. In 1549 he was freed and went to England, where he was a pastor first in the north and later as a chaplain for King Edward VI. However when Queen Mary of England became queen in 1553, he had to flee from England. John Knox went to Calvin's Geneva. For part of this time he was the pastor of English-speaking exiles in Geneva.

John Knox was very impressed with Calvin's Geneva, calling it "the most perfect school of Christ that ever was in the earth since the days of the Apostles." He felt that Christ was truly preached elsewhere, but the manners and religion in Geneva were "sincerely reformed." When Knox left Geneva, he was a convinced Calvinist.

In 1559, Knox returned to his native Scotland, arriving in Edinburgh, the capital, on May 2. The time was ripe for his return. Two years earlier a group of Scottish nobles had signed the "First Covenant," which was a commitment to renounce the Roman Catholic Church and set up a national Protestant church. But Mary of Lorraine, who was the regent (acting ruler), was actively promoting the Roman Catholic cause. When Knox arrived in Scotland, he went from town to town preaching the Protestant message. A fiery preacher, Knox knew how to stir up the people. He was also a man of prayer. His constant prayer to God was: "Give me Scotland, or I die."

The next year, on June 11, 1560, the regent died. Scotland's next queen, Mary Queen of Scots, was in France, which was her mother's country. The Parliament took advantage of the absence of a king or queen to declare Scotland a Protestant country.

In August of 1560 the Scottish Parliament abolished the authority of the pope and forbade the celebration of the Latin Mass. Roman Catholicism was officially banned in Scotland by Parliament. The same Parliament called on John Knox and five others to draw up a Confession of Faith, a Book of Common Order and a Book of Discipline.

The First Scottish Confession was drawn up and adopted by Parliament in August 17, 1560. This Confession was a clear statement of the Reformed faith. It was the doctrinal standard of the Church of Scotland until the Westminster Confession replaced it in 1647. The Reformed faith was now the official religion of Scotland.

The Book of Common Order was approved by the General Assembly of the Church of Scotland. It is also known as Knox's liturgy. It was a guide for the conduct of ordinary and special worship services. This Book was used by the Church for a hundred years.

The First Book of Discipline regulated the life of the Church of Scotland for at least a century. It called for the celebration of the Lord's Supper four times a year. It recognized five church offices: minister, lay reader, superintendent, elder and deacon. The lay readers were supposed to lead services in the absence of a pastor. The deacons were elected annually, and were responsible for matters of finance. The elders were elected annually and were assistants to the minister. The superintendents were in charge of districts, but were not bishops.

The Book of Discipline called for a comprehensive scheme of education in the country in order to improve the lot of the people. It also called for a system of church discipline in order to improve the spiritual quality of the lives of the people.

Thus by 1560 Scotland had become a very Presbyterian country. This had happened very rapidly after the return of John Knox in 1559. However, the gains that had been made were soon threatened by the return to Scotland of its young queen, Mary Stuart, Queen of Scots, in 1561. On the Sunday after her return she had the Mass celebrated in her castle in Edinburgh. Nearby, in the main church, the church of St. Giles, John Knox preached strongly against this violation of Parliament's decision. The war between John Knox, preacher of the Word, and Mary Queen of Scots had begun!

Mary was only eighteen years old, attractive, impulsive, and a devout Roman Catholic. John Knox was stern, a powerful preacher, and Reformed. His pulpit in St. Giles church was just up the road from the Holyrood Castle. At first Mary proceeded with caution. She appointed a number of Protestant nobles and advisers to serve in the government. But soon she began to make mistakes. She married one man, but later possibly caused his death. Then she turned around and married another man, Lord Bothwell, after he hurriedly divorced his wife to marry the queen. Both the Catholics and Protestants in Scotland turned against her, and she became a prisoner in 1567. She spent the last twenty years of her life in prison in England.

With Mary's fall, Presbyterianism was established in Scotland. When John Knox died in 1572, Andrew Melville defended the Presbyterian system against King James VI (James I of England). The Scottish Presbyterians gave important support to the Puritans in England in the seventeenth century. When the Westminster Confession and Catechisms were written in 1646 and 1647, the Church of Scotland adopted them as their doctrinal standards. The

Church of Scotland today is the main church in Scotland, and it still reflects the influence of Calvin and John Knox.

England

The country of England to the south of Scotland also had important Reformed influences. The Reformation came to England when its king, Henry VIII, who reigned from 1509 to 1547, decided to throw off the authority of the pope. The king was Roman Catholic in his theology, but he wanted to be rid of the pope so that he could get a divorce.

During Henry's reign Protestant ideas began to enter England. William Tyndale's translation of the Bible into English in 1526 brought the Bible into the language and hands of the people. Luther's ideas were coming into the country through books written by Luther and by English Christians.

The ideas of Calvin began to influence England towards the end of Henry's reign. During the 1540s Calvin was becoming more well-known and appreciated. But the significant time of change came when Henry's son became king. Edward VI, who reigned from 1547 to 1553, was only nine years old when he began to reign. A nobleman, the Duke of Somerset or Protector Somerset, ruled for Edward in the first years of his reign. Both Edward and Somerset were very sympathetic to the ideas of Calvin.

During Edward's reign, many theologians in the country were beginning to read Calvin's writings. So in 1553 the Church of England and the King approved the 42 Articles, which were Calvinist in their theology but not in the liturgy.

Edward died at the age of 15. His sister, Mary Tudor, who reigned from 1553 to 1558, became queen at the age of 37. Mary was a convinced Roman Catholic and began by persecuting and executing some of the Protestants, including

Archbishop Cranmer. Hence she has often been called Bloody Mary.

Because of the danger, many English Protestants fled to Germany and Switzerland. Many refugees, such as John Knox, went to Geneva to find safety. This was the time when Calvin's influence was strong in Geneva. Many of these exiles became convinced of Calvin's teachings. So in God's providence some good things came to the church of England despite the persecution.

When Mary died in 1558 and her sister Elizabeth became queen, many of these exiles returned to England with their Reformed ideas. Queen Elizabeth I, who reigned from 1558 to 1603, was a moderate Protestant. The Elizabethan Settlement was an attempt to satisfy both sides. Roman Catholicism was rejected, and so was extreme Presbyterianism. Elizabeth retained the archbishops and bishops, and the priests wore the old Catholic vestments. But the theology of the Church of England at this time was Calvinistic.

During the reign of Elizabeth, Puritanism appeared as a new movement. The Puritans were those Reformed Christians who tried to purify the Church of England. They were generally Calvinist in doctrine; they were also opposed to episcopal church government (government by bishops) and they favored simpler practices in worship.

In the next century the Puritans were opposed by King James I (1603-1625) and King Charles I (1625-1649) in England. However during the 1640s a Parliament with strong Presbyterian leanings was in power. It was during this time that the Westminster Assembly was convened. This is the Assembly that produced the Westminster Confession in 1646 and the Larger and Shorter Westminster Catechisms in 1647. The Shorter Catechism, which was written mainly for the education of children, opens with the beautiful question and answer: "What is the chief end of man? Man's chief end is to glorify God, and to enjoy him forever." This question and answer is an admirable summary of the Reformed faith.

Although the official church in England was the Anglican church, Presbyterians received religious freedom in 1689 when a Toleration Act gave freedom of worship to non-Anglican Protestants.

In the seventeenth century the Puritans wrote many theological and devotional books in the Reformed tradition. Puritan theology emphasizes the personal Christian life. The Puritans taught the doctrine of election, but they were also keen to find fruits of election in the life of the Christian. *Pilgrim's Progress* is a book written by John Bunyan which is a classic example of Puritan writing. It shows how the Christian life is like a journey to heaven and how a Christian must rely on God through prayer and the reading of the Bible to avoid the temptations in life and to remain faithful to Christ. The Puritans helped keep Reformed theology practical for the Christian.

In the last two centuries there has not been a large Reformed church in England, but there have been Reformed church leaders and lay people within existing English churches. We will cite only one example. A great Calvinist was Charles Haddon Spurgeon (1834-1892). Spurgeon was the greatest preacher in England at that time. He preached in the specially erected Metropolitan Tabernacle, which seated 6000 people. It is interesting to note that Spurgeon, although Reformed was also a Baptist. We could call Spurgeon a Reformed Baptist, for he was Reformed in his theology although he did not practice infant baptism. Today there are some Reformed Baptist churches in England and America, as well as in Nigeria. The Qua Iboe Church and the Evangelical Reformed Church of Christ are Reformed Baptist.

Study Questions

1. Who were the Catholics in Scotland that opposed the Protestant faith?
2. How did Reformed ideas come to Scotland?
3. Identify three Marys in English and Scottish history. What did they do?
4. List four English kings and queens of the sixteenth century. Which ones were Catholic and which ones Protestant?
5. Why did the Puritans disagree with the Church of England?
6. What is a Reformed Baptist?

Chapter Four

Reformed Churches in France, Germany and Eastern Europe

The influence of Calvin was international. We have just seen how Calvinism came to Scotland and England, which are part of the British Isles. This chapter will look at the Reformed churches on the continent of Europe, across the water from Britain. We will look especially at France, Germany and Eastern Europe. In the next chapter we will look at Holland.

France

It is natural that Calvin's ideas should spread in France since Calvin was born and raised as a Frenchman. Since Calvin wrote in French as well as Latin, his people could read his books in their own language. Also many French people came to Geneva and learned about Calvin's ideas.

It is therefore tragic that the Reformed church in France usually suffered persecution. Starting in 1533 there was serious persecution of Protestants in France. Therefore many French people came to Geneva to seek safety. In 1536 the population of Geneva was around ten thousand; by 1564 ten thousand refugees, mostly from France, had moved into the city. Some of these refugees studied in Geneva to be pastors. When they finished their education, they went back to France to pastor Reformed churches.

In 1555 there were five Reformed churches in France. Four years later, in 1559, there were one hundred Reformed churches. Most of these churches had to meet secretly, often in a person's house, for fear of persecution.

In 1559, the Reformed churches in France had their first Synod meeting, in Paris, the capital. This meeting was held in secret for fear of persecution. About half of the hundred churches sent delegates. At this meeting a Confession of Faith and a Form of Discipline were adopted. The Reformed Church in France had four levels of government: the local consistory; the colloquy, which supervised a number of congregations; the provincial synod; and the national synod, which met annually. The annual synod was made up of two ministers and two elders from each of the provincial synods. By 1562 the number of Reformed congregations in France had risen to 2,150 churches. Clearly the church was growing rapidly.

But the Reformed church met opposition from the king and the government. The most shocking event was the St. Bartholomew's Day Massacre, so called because it occurred on that special day. On this day the Roman Catholics killed tens of thousands of Reformed Christians throughout France. After that there were seven civil wars between the Catholics and Reformed Protestants between 1562 and 1580.

The Reformed Christians in France were called Huguenots. In 1598 King Henry IV enacted a law giving the Huguenots freedom of worship, but this edict was revoked in 1685, and about a half a million Huguenot Christians fled to other European countries. France clearly lost some of its best people at this time. After 1685 the Reformed church continued to exist in France, but it was small and often persecuted. Today France is a nominally Catholic country, with only a few Protestant churches.

Germany

East of France is the country of Germany. Today Germany is one country, but in the sixteenth century it was a group of many small kingdoms and free cities. Lutheranism was strong in Germany since Luther was German and wrote in the German language. However there were a few kingdoms and cities that accepted the Reformed faith. Most notable was the city of Heidelberg, the most important city of the Lower Palatinate, which was a German kingdom. The prince or king in Heidelberg, Frederick III (1559-1576), became a Calvinist in 1560.

Frederick brought a number of Reformed theologians into his kingdom, including an eloquent preacher, Caspar Olevianus, and a professor of theology, Zacharias Ursinus. Frederick asked them to prepare a Reformed catechism for his kingdom, and the result was the famous Heidelberg Catechism, completed in 1563.

This catechism, written for Heidelberg, was quickly accepted by Reformed churches throughout Europe. The Heidelberg Catechism is one of the greatest documents of the Reformed tradition. It is written in a very pastoral and personal way, applying the Reformed doctrines to the life of the Christian. Its division into the three parts of sin, salvation and service (or guilt, grace and gratitude) is a very helpful way of understanding the Christian life. Its opening question and answer are a fine illustration of the pastoral quality of this catechism: "What is your only comfort in life and in death? That I am not my own, but belong--body and soul, in life and in death--to my faithful Savior Jesus Christ."

The Heidelberg Catechism is used today by at least four Reformed churches in Nigeria (CRCN, RCCN, NKST and RCN). It is a classic statement of our Reformed faith.

Eastern Europe

In Eastern Europe, Calvinism made some impact, but not all of it was lasting. In **Poland** the Reformed faith made its greatest headway during the reign of King Sigismund II (Augustus) (1548-1572). The King corresponded with Calvin and he had read the *Institutes* with admiration. We still have the texts of letters that Calvin wrote to King Sigismund, urging him to bow the knee to Jesus and to establish the Kingdom of Christ in Poland. In the end, however, Sigismund did not become Protestant. When the Catholic Jesuits came into Poland in 1564, the Protestant churches eventually collapsed. Today Poland is a strongly Roman Catholic country, the home of Pope John Paul II.

Hungary is the one country of Eastern Europe that still has a significant Reformed church. The history of the Hungarian church and people is one of persecution. Hungary was located between the Hapsburg empire, which was Roman Catholic, and the Turkish empire, which was Muslim. Both Lutheranism and Calvinism came to Hungary early, and eventually there were both Lutheran and Reformed churches. Both churches were persecuted from time to time, both by the Roman Catholics and the Muslims, but by God's grace both churches have survived up to this time.
When Hungary and Germany lost the First World War (1914-1918), some of Hungary's land was given to neighboring countries. Today there are Hungarian-speaking Reformed churches in Romania as well as in Hungary. The Reformed churches suffered under Communist rule in the twentieth century, but by God's grace they survived. In the late 1980s, it was a Reformed Hungarian pastor who began the revolt against Communism in Romania.

Study Questions

1. What is a Huguenot?
2. How are the histories of the Reformed churches in France and Poland similar?
3. What is the first question and answer of the Heidelberg Catechism?
4. Describe the similarities and differences of the Reformed movement in Hungary and Poland.
5. Identify Henry IV, Frederick III and Sigismund Augustus.
6. Identify Caspar Olevianus and Zacharias Ursinus.

Chapter Five

Reformed Churches in the Netherlands

The Netherlands, or Holland, is a small country in the northwest of Europe. It is important for Nigerian history because the CRCN, RCCN, NKST and NRC have been influenced by its theology.

The Dutch Reformation

At the time of Calvin, the Netherlands was a larger country than today, comprising both Belgium and Holland. At the beginning of the sixteenth century, the Netherlands and Germany were ruled by the Emperor Charles V. He reigned from 1519 to 1555. This is the same Emperor before whom Martin Luther appeared at the Diet of Worms in 1521, when he is thought to have said: "Here I stand." On his return from the city of Worms to the Netherlands, Charles forbade the reading of Luther's works. Soon Protestants were dying for their faith.

The ideas of Luther and Calvin had come to the Netherlands early, and they found a good reception. The Dutch people were a sturdy, freedom-loving people, and the Calvinistic ideas of self-government appealed to them. They resented the restrictions that were placed upon their faith. Soon the Reformed faith was the main Protestant religion in the Netherlands.

In 1561 a Reformed Christian, Guy (or Guido) de Bres, wrote a confession of faith "for the faithful who are everywhere scattered through the Netherlands." This confession was called the Belgic Confession because it was written in the south of the Netherlands, which is present-day Belgium. It is a basic summary of the Reformed faith, and it became the main statement of faith for the Calvinists in the Netherlands.

In 1555 Charles V stepped down from the throne, and his son, Philip II, became king of Spain and the Netherlands. Philip ruled the Netherlands from his palace in Spain from 1555 to 1598. He was both a foreign king and a Roman Catholic, who suppressed the Reformed faith.

A great struggle then broke out between Philip and the Dutch people. The Dutch people, who were rapidly becoming Calvinist, resented his rule. So in 1568 the Dutch provinces revolted against the Spanish.

The struggle between the Dutch and the Spanish lasted for 80 years, from 1568 to 1648, although the most intensive fighting was in the first 25 years. The Spanish duke of Alva brutally tried to suppress the Dutch people, but the Dutch resisted under the leadership of William the Silent. The Reformed faith was associated with the movement for freedom, and the Reformed churches grew during this time. By 1592 it was clear that the Dutch would win, but it was not until 1648 that Holland was recognized as a country independent of Spain.

The Synod of Dort

The seventeenth century in Holland was a time of prosperity. The Dutch were good merchants, and their trading ships went throughout the world. At this time the Reformed church in Holland was also strong.

During this time of apparent security, a serious disagreement arose in the Reformed church on doctrinal matters. The controversy started with a pastor and professor, Jacob Arminius (1560-1609). Arminius had been a student of Theodore Beza in Geneva and then in 1588 he became a Reformed pastor in the Dutch city of Amsterdam.

In 1603 Arminius became professor at the University of Leiden. While he was professor, it became evident that he did not agree with the traditional Reformed doctrine of election. Arminius died in 1609, but there were 43 pastors who followed his teachings. In 1610 they set forth their beliefs, summarized in five points: 1) God did not elect individuals but only the group of those who believe; 2) Christ died for all people; 3) faith is a gift of God; 4) but the gift of faith is resistible; 5) they were uncertain about the doctrine of perseverance. These are the Five Points of Arminianism.

Because these beliefs were causing problems in the church, the Dutch government called an international synod to deal with the matter. This synod, which was held in the Dutch city of Dordrecht, is called the Synod of Dort. It met from November 1618 to May 1619. In addition to the Dutch delegates, there were delegates from the Reformed churches in England, Germany, and Switzerland. The conclusions of the Synod are the Canons of Dort. They are summarized by the Five Points of Calvinism, which were a response to the five points of the Arminians. The Five Points of Calvinism are: 1) God elected believers before the foundation of the world; 2) Christ's death is sufficient for all but efficient only for the elect; 3) fallen man is totally unable to save himself; 4) salvation is the gift of the irresistible work of the Holy Spirit; 5) God preserves the elect so that they do not fall away from grace.

The Synod of Dort

In this synod, Dutch Calvinism reaffirmed the teachings of Calvin and Beza. The Canons of Dort, together with the Heidelberg Catechism and the Belgic Confession, has become the doctrinal basis for many Reformed churches.

Seventeenth-century theology in Holland, as in Puritan England, had a special concern for Christian piety. Reformed theology was not just an intellectual belief; it was also concerned about the Christian life. Dutch theologians began to write and teach about these issues especially after the Synod of Dort.

The (Dutch) Christian Reformed Church[1]

The eighteenth century in Europe was called the Age of Reason. Rationalism, or an extreme use of reason, came into the Reformed church. For example, one Reformed theological professor in Holland denied the deity of Christ, the fall of Adam and Eve, eternal punishment and the atonement, because he thought these doctrines were "unreasonable." Such theologians placed reason above the Bible.

In 1816 the new Dutch King, William I, imposed a church order on the Reformed church which was hierarchical instead of presbyterian. The Dutch government interfered in the affairs of the church. (This is the same problem that Calvin had faced in Geneva.)

During this time there was a spiritual revival throughout Europe called the Awakening or Revival. This revival also came to Holland. There were many people in the Reformed church who were not happy with the theology and

---

[1] See chapter 6 for the story of the Christian Reformed Church in North America.

the apparent spiritual deadness in the church and with the state interference in the church.

In 1834 some of these Christians left the original Reformed church; these people were called the Secessionists. In 1836 they formed the Christian Reformed Church. Because of persecution in Holland, two of their pastors led some of their members to America, where in 1857 they founded the Christian Reformed Church, a sister church to the Dutch one.

However not all of the members concerned for revival left the original Reformed Church. Perhaps the most famous of these was Abraham Kuyper (1837-1921). After getting his doctorate in 1862, Kuyper first became a pastor in a Reformed church in Utrecht. Then in 1870 he became pastor in one of the churches in Amsterdam. During these pastorates he became concerned about the theological and spiritual life of the Reformed church and he worked for reform.

Kuyper was of a different mold than the Secessionists of 1834. Whereas the Secessionists were pietistic (concerned with personal Christian spirituality), Kuyper believed that Christianity should not be restricted to the personal life but should include all of life. Kuyper believed strongly in the lordship or sovereignty of Christ over all of life. He expressed this conviction powerfully in the following words: "There is not a single square inch of the entire universe of which Christ the sovereign Lord of all does not say, 'This is mine!'"[2] Kuyper was clearly concerned about personal Christian spirituality; yet he also realized that Christianity involved far more than just individual piety.

Kuyper put these principles into practice. In 1872 he began to edit a daily newspaper, *The Standard*, in which he

---

[2]Quoted by Gordon Spykman in *Reformational Theology* (Grand Rapids, 1992), p. 474.

was able to develop Christian principles for society. In 1874 he was elected to be a member of Parliament, although this meant retiring from the pastorate. While in Parliament, he established a Christian political party, the Anti-Revolutionary Party. In 1880 he helped found the Free University of Amsterdam, which was established upon Christian principles. From 1901 to 1905 he was the prime minister of Holland. As prime minister he worked to get governmental financial support for Christian schools, and he also worked for social legislation to protect working people. During this time he also wrote theological articles and books. Clearly Kuyper believed that Christ should be Lord over all of life, and he attempted to put this into practice.

While engaged in all of these activities, Kuyper was an elder in his local church in Amsterdam. In 1886 he and most of his consistory came into disagreement with the old Reformed Church about issues of doctrine, so Kuyper's church and about 200 other churches left the denomination. In 1892 they joined with some of the Secessionist churches to found the Reformed Churches in the Netherlands.

Netherlands Reformed Congregations

Another Reformed church arose in Holland at this time. This church is important for Nigeria because they are now working in the Izi area in the east of Nigeria. This denomination is the Netherlands Reformed Congregations (NRC). This church was founded in 1907.

The NRC in Holland emphasizes the practical dimension of the Reformed faith. They teach the holiness of God and the sinfulness of man. They believe that every person must have a deep knowledge of his own sin before he comes to salvation. They emphasize the personal experience that is necessary for true conversion. A true Christian must be able to explain his conversion experience. The fruits of the Spirit must be evident in the life of a true believer.

The NRC assumes that the majority of the people in a church still lack true heart conversion. Therefore, when the Lord's Supper is celebrated, most of the people in the church do not partake of it.

The NRC in Holland teaches that the Christian must separate himself from the world. They teach that believers must not own televisions; they must not dance; and they must avoid modern fashions and materialism in general.

The NRC is a conservative Reformed church. They try to apply the Reformed doctrines to the Christian's life. They emphasize separation from the world more than transformation of the world. They reject many of the teachings of Abraham Kuyper.

Study questions

1. Why did the Dutch fight a war against Spain? When was this war?
2. What are the Belgic Confession and the Canons of Dort? When were they written?
3. How did Arminius disagree with Calvin's theology?
4. What are the decisions of the Synod of Dort?
5. When and why was the Christian Reformed Church in Holland formed?
6. What is the most important belief of Abraham Kuyper?
7. What are the most important beliefs of the Netherlands Reformed Congregations?

Chapter Six

North America and South Africa

The spread of the Reformed movement from Europe to other continents occurred as a result of exploration, trade and immigration. In the 1400s the coast of Africa was being explored by Portuguese ships and in 1492 Christopher Columbus discovered North America. These discoveries occurred before Martin Luther's Reformation, which began in 1517.

Thus before 1600 it was the Catholic nations of Portugal, Spain and France that evangelized parts of Africa and America. After 1600 their power declined, and England and Holland, which were Protestant, became world powers.

Between 1600 and 1900, Reformed churches were founded in North America, South Africa, Australia, New Zealand, Indonesia and Sri Lanka, to name a few. Many of these churches were established as a result of immigration.

In this chapter we will look briefly at North America and South Africa.

North America

The Europeans discovered America in 1492. In the 1500s, some French and Spanish Catholics immigrated to America. Protestant immigration began after 1600 when English and Dutch ships were crossing the seas.

In the 1620s and 1630s, when the Puritans were being denied religious freedom in England, thousands of English

Puritans came to New England, in the northeast of America. They were Calvinist in their theology but congregationalist instead of presbyterian in their church polity. In other words, they believed that each local congregation was essentially autonomous and they did not have presbyteries or synods. Harvard College and Yale College (now universities) were founded by Calvinists for the training of their ministers. The New England Congregationalist churches were Reformed in theology during the 1600s.

South of New England, in present-day New York City, the Dutch settled at this time. They called their new settlement New Amsterdam. They established a Reformed church there, which later became the Reformed Church of America. In 1664 the English took control of New Amsterdam and called it New York, but the Reformed church continued in this English colony.

In the 1600s many Scottish Presbyterians had immigrated to northern Ireland. In the 1700s they experienced religious discrimination from the English government, and about 250,000 Scotch-Irish came to America. Many of these people were strongly Presbyterian, and it was through their influence that the Presbyterian church in America was formed. The first American presbytery was formed in Philadelphia in 1706, and the Synod of Philadelphia was formed in 1717. The College of New Jersey (now Princeton Seminary and University) was founded by the Presbyterians in 1755 for the training of their pastors.

The Presbyterians have always been a major religious force in American society. Because of their concern for religious freedom, the Presbyterians were strongly in support of the War of Independence from England in 1776. Many Presbyterian values have influenced American society. Today there are two larger and many smaller Presbyterian denominations in America. There is also a Presbyterian church in Canada.

We have already seen that the Reformed Church of America had its roots in the Dutch immigration to New York in the early 1600s. Later in the nineteenth century there were other waves of Dutch immigration to America. The first significant immigration was that of the Secessionists under the leadership of Rev. A. Van Raalte and Rev. H. Scholte. (We already discussed the Secessionists in the chapter on Holland.) In 1847 Rev. Van Raalte led a group of these Reformed Christians across the ocean and they founded the town of Holland in Michigan. Holland is about 50 miles west of Grand Rapids, Michigan. In the same year Rev. Scholte led other Reformed believers and established the town of Pella in southeast Iowa. They started churches which first associated with the Reformed Church of America; but in 1857 they left this church and founded the Christian Reformed Church.

This first wave of immigration was the doctrinal-pietistic branch of the Reformed faith: in other words they were concerned with orthodox theology and individual piety. Then after 1870 a new wave of immigration came from the Netherlands to the Christian Reformed Church. These immigrants were influenced by the worldview of Abraham Kuyper. In addition to a concern for orthodox doctrine and individual piety, they advocated a Calvinism concerned about transforming culture. They strongly emphasized the belief that Christ is sovereign over all of life and society.

The Christian Reformed Church today reflects these three elements of Dutch Calvinism: a concern for personal piety, an adherence to the traditional Reformed creeds, and a belief in the transforming power of Christ in all of society. It is of course clear that not all Christian Reformed members, including missionaries, will emphasize these elements equally.

Some members feel more concerned about doctrine; others about personal salvation; others about culture. A wholistic Christian, however, will be equally concerned with all three.

South Africa

In the seventeenth century, when the Reformed faith was being brought to America through immigration, a Reformed settlement also occurred in South Africa. This settlement happened at the time when the Dutch ships were exploring and colonizing parts of the world.

The history of the Dutch and Reformed influence in South Africa is a tragic one. The Dutch Reformed Christians often did not apply their beliefs to their relations with the African people. Clearly the rule of Christ was not always allowed to shine in these relations. Thankfully, however, there were moments of grace in this history.

South Africa is a multi-tribal country in which the Zulus are one of the most well-known tribes. The first Europeans to settle in South Africa worked for the Dutch East India Company. This company had ships which went from Holland around Africa to Indonesia. They established a station in 1652 in what is now Cape Town to supply provisions of food and water for their ships. Soon some of these Dutch people began to settle in and around Cape Town. Many of these first Europeans were Reformed, and Reformed churches were established from the start.

A Dutch person in South Africa was called a Boer, which means farmer. The relation between the Boers and the Africans went through different phases. At times they coexisted peacefully, but in 1836 the Boers migrated north into Zulu country, and in 1838 there was the tragic Battle of Blood River when many Zulus were killed.

Yet there was also significant evangelism of the African people. J.T. van der Kemp was a Reformed Christian who married an African and worked as a missionary among the Xhosa people. The first Xhosa Christian, Ntsikana, was converted through his preaching. Ntsikana, in turn, was used by God in the conversion of Tiyo Soga, who became the first black South African to be ordained into the ministry, as a Presbyterian pastor.

The Dutch Reformed Church (NGK) in South Africa was active in evangelism outside of South Africa as well. The Dutch Reformed Church Mission (DRCM) came to places like Nigeria in the twentieth century. It was the DRCM that worked among the Tiv people in the early twentieth century.

Unfortunately, though, already in the nineteenth century, blacks and whites began to worship separately. Apartheid, which did not become law until the 20th century, was already being practiced by some Christians in the 19th century. Yet it was not until the 1940s and early 1950s that apartheid as an official system became law. (The word apartheid means separateness in the Afrikaans language.) To the shame of the white Dutch Reformed Church many of their members supported apartheid and too often refused to criticize it.

However there were some Reformed Christians, both black and white, who opposed apartheid. Dr. Allan Boesak is a black Reformed pastor and theologian who was vigorous in his opposition to apartheid. Dr. Boesak also served as president of the World Alliance of Reformed Churches in the 1980s. Dr. C.F. Beyers Naude was a white Reformed pastor who was also vocal in his opposition to apartheid and who lived a life of love to his African brothers and sisters. Partly due to the efforts of people like this, apartheid as a legal system was finally abolished in 1994.

Study questions

1. Describe how European persecution resulted in the formation of three American churches.
2. Describe the origins of the Presbyterian churches in America.
3. Describe three theological emphases in the Christian Reformed Church.
4. How did the Dutch Reformed people in South Africa not practice their Reformed theology?
5. Name two Reformed opponents of apartheid in South Africa.
6. Identify Van Raalte, Ntsikana and Tiyo Soga.

Chapter Seven

Presbyterian and Reformed Churches in Southern Nigeria

The nineteenth century was the great era of the expansion of the church. During this century the Gospel was brought to almost every country of the world.

The 1840s were a decisive decade for Nigerian Christianity, for this is when Protestant Christianity first came to Nigeria. In this decade the Anglicans, Methodists, Presbyterians and Baptists (who actually came in 1850) each began a major mission in Nigeria. At this time Samuel Crowther returned to his home as a member of the Anglican mission. In these significant years the first Reformed witness in Nigeria was heard through the Presbyterian church.

This chapter will look at three Reformed and Presbyterian churches that were founded in the south of Nigeria: the Presbyterian Church of Nigeria, the Qua Iboe Church and the Nigeria Reformed Church.

Presbyterian Church of Nigeria

It is noteworthy that the impetus to bring the Gospel to Calabar came from a church composed of both Africans and Europeans. This church was on the island of Jamaica, which is located in the Caribbean Sea near Central America.

There was a large number of African slaves in Jamaica at this time. By the Act of 1833, the British Parliament freed all of these slaves. Many of these Africans had come from what is now Nigeria, and they wanted to bring the Gospel to their own people. In 1841 the Jamaica Mission Presbytery requested the Scottish Missionary Society, which had begun the work in Jamaica, to send missionaries from Jamaica to West Africa. However the Scottish missionary society thought the proposal was too bold, and they turned it down.

The following year the Presbytery repeated its request. By now there were Christians in Scotland who were also interested in such a venture. The chiefs of Calabar were contacted through the captains of British trading vessels, and King Eyamba and King Eyo Honesty both wrote that missionaries were welcome. King Eyamba wrote: "Plenty sugar cane live here, and if some man come teach we way for do it we get plenty sugar too, and then some man must come for teach book proper, and make all men saby [know] God like white man." Both kings agreed that the time of slave trade was over and they wanted to trade in sugar and other commodities with the British.

So the Jamaica Presbytery sent Rev. Hope Masterton Waddell, a missionary in Jamaica, to Scotland to make negotiations. By this time the Scottish churches were interested in the project, and the United Secession Church adopted the new mission. Mr. Robert Jamieson, a Liverpool trader, offered the use of the ship *Warree* and some cash for the mission.

On January 6, 1846, the pioneering party set sail from Liverpool in the *Warree*. The mission party consisted of six people: Rev. Hope Waddell; Mr. Samuel Edgerley, who was a printer; his wife; Andrew Chisholm, a carpenter, of mixed race; Edward Miller, a Jamaican teacher of African descent; and a young man, George, who was an ex-slave. At the beginning of April they landed on the island of Fernando Po; on April 10, 1846, they arrived in Duke Town, Old Calabar.

The missionaries were welcomed first by King Eyo Honesty of Creek Town, and then by King Eyamba the Fifth of Duke Town, "King of all Black Men," as he called himself. The missionaries were given three sites to build mission stations: one in Duke Town, one in Creek Town and one in Old Town. It was in Creek Town that the Gospel made the greatest progress. King Eyo Honesty gave a building for a school and encouraged it by his own presence. On Sunday, services were held in his compound, and the king himself acted as interpreter. Although Eyo was never baptized, his son, also called Eyo, was baptized in 1853.

Two weeks before young Eyo's baptism, Esien Esien Ukpabio was baptized publicly in King Eyo's yard. He was the first person to be baptized in Calabar and he was also to be the first native teacher and the first African pastor in this city. In the same year others were baptized in Duke Town and Old Town.

The mission work was slow, but by God's grace there was fruit. The missionaries fought against practices like the killing of twins and also the killing of slaves when an important man died. A major triumph occurred at the time of the death of King Eyo Honesty in 1858, for by his instructions no slaves were put to death.

The young church was displaying maturity. In 1856 when Hope Waddell left Nigeria, the church in Creek Town sent a gift of 71 pounds sterling for mission work. On September 1, 1858, the Presbytery of Biafra was formed. In 1872 Esien Esien Ukpabio was ordained to the ministry.

The church also spread beyond Calabar. The printer, Samuel Edgerley, explored new areas, bringing the Gospel. Others followed his example. Perhaps the best known missionary to spread the Gospel in this area was a young lady

Mary Mitchell Slessor

from Scotland, Miss Mary Mitchell Slessor. At the age of 28 she came to Africa, working first in Duke Town. She longed to be sent into the interior to work. In 1888 she went to Okoyong, where she did medical work, preached the Gospel, and also became involved in settling disputes between local chiefs and clans. In 1896 she moved with the Okoyong people to Akpap; after 1903 she began to work in the area of Arochukwu, the home of the Long Juju, settling in 1904 in Itu. This remarkable woman was taken to be with the Lord on January 13, 1915, at the age of 66. She had given her life to Africa, and the Lord blessed her labors. In 1921 the Synod of Biafra was constituted; on October 19, 1945, almost a century after the beginning of the work in Calabar, it was called the Presbyterian Church of Biafra. The name was changed later to the Presbyterian Church of Eastern Nigeria, and in 1960 it became the Presbyterian Church of Nigeria (PCN).

Due to an agreement reached at the World Missionary Conference held in Edinburgh in 1910, the Presbyterian missionary activity was originally restricted to the southeast of Nigeria, in particular the lower and upper Cross River areas. Gradually however the church expanded beyond this region. As indigenes from eastern Nigeria migrated to other parts of the country, Presbyterian churches were established in these places. In 1977 the Presbytery of the North was founded; in recent years church planting among the Tiv and the Yoruba has started. A new work on the Mambilla Plateau has also begun.

The Presbyterian Church of Nigeria trains its pastors and church leaders at Trinity College, Umuahia; Presbyterian Theological College, Itu; Presbyterian Seminary, Ohafia; as well as the Theological College of Northern Nigeria, Bukuru.

At present there are at least 20 presbyteries and more than 250 parishes. There are at least 250 ministers, including some women pastors. The first woman minister was ordained in 1982.

Qua Iboe Church

The Qua Iboe church does not call itself Reformed or Presbyterian, but in most points of doctrine and practice it is. Its *Manual of Doctrine and Practice* is evangelical in its teaching, and in particular affirms the authority of the Bible, the sovereignty of God, and the primary role of the Holy Spirit in causing salvation. Its doctrine of eternal security is also Reformed. Its church polity is basically Presbyterian since it teaches that the church is ruled by elders; its second basic office is that of deacon.

The only point in which they differ from most Reformed churches is on the issue of baptism. They practice believers' baptism and not infant baptism. In this sense, they are quite close to the Reformed Baptist position.

The founder of the Qua Iboe Church was from a Presbyterian background. Rev. Samuel Bill was a native of Northern Ireland and a product of the Presbyterian community there. The Presbyterians in Northern Ireland have their roots in Scotland; many of them are ethnically of Scottish background. The headquarters of the Qua Iboe Mission (now called the Qua Iboe Fellowship) is still located in Belfast, Northern Ireland.

The initiative for another mission in the southeast of Nigeria came from some local chiefs among the people of Ibeno, a village at the mouth of the Qua Iboe River. In the mid-1800s, the Ibeno people had been attacked by fifty war canoes equipped with cannons from a neighboring village. Fearing another attack, the Ibeno chiefs suggested that they request a white teacher to come and live with them. They hoped that the presence of a white man might prevent a future attack. They asked a British trader to write a letter and send it to the Scottish Presbyterian mission.

The Scottish mission did not have the personnel to meet this request, so they passed the letter on to Dr. Grattan Guinness, the principal of the Harley Missionary Training College in London. One day in June 1887, after the evening meal, Dr. Guinness stood up before all the students and read the letter. He asked whether one of them would be interested in serving the Lord among the Ibeno. Samuel Alexander Bill was a young man from Belfast who was a student at the College. When he heard Dr. Guinness's invitation, he felt that this call was being directed to him. First of all he spent some time in prayer; then he talked with some Christian friends. After a few days he went to the principal and said that he was offering to answer the call in that letter, with God's help. Some weeks later a cheque of one hundred pounds came to cover his passage to West Africa. This served as a confirmation that this was the will of God.

As Samuel Bill was preparing to travel, he met a young English lady by the name of Grace Kerr. They agreed to get married but not until he had first traveled alone to Africa for the first time. On September 14, 1887, he departed from Liverpool, and on October 6 he arrived in Calabar, where he received assistance and advice from Presbyterian missionaries. Early in 1888 he took a small steamer from Calabar to the fishing village of Ibeno.

"Etubom" Samuel Bill settled in Ibeno, completed the house that was started for him, and began preaching the Gospel. Soon a friend from Ireland, Mr. Archie Baillie, joined him in his work. The first convert was a son of a prominent chief and grandson of the High Priest of Ekong, David Ekong. Early on he showed interest in the Gospel, and he soon confessed his faith in Jesus and was baptized. Later Ekong became pastor of the Ibeno church and one of the pioneer leaders of the Qua Iboe Church.

In 1890 Samuel Bill returned home and married Grace Kerr. They returned a year later, and Grace Bill proved to be a valuable help to her husband and to the new church, despite frequent health problems. God blessed this church and it spread throughout the southeast of Nigeria. In 1928 a spiritual revival swept through the church. One of the results of this revival was the desire to bring the Gospel to other parts of Nigeria. At the first Qua Iboe conference in Ibeno in 1930 the decision was taken to take the Gospel to the Igala people. From this decision and with the help of the Holy Spirit a strong arm of the Qua Iboe church can be found in Igalaland today.

Mr. Bill and his wife committed their lives to the Qua Iboe Church. Bill was 25 years old when he came to Ibeno, and he spent 54 years in Nigeria. He died at the age of 79 in 1942 and was buried on Ibeno soil behind the church building next to his wife. The Qua Iboe Church recognized his invaluable contribution to their lives by naming their theological seminary after him. The Samuel Bill Theological College is located in Abak, Akwa Ibom State.

Nigeria Reformed Church

The third Reformed church to be started in the south of Nigeria is a small and recent one. The Nigeria Reformed Church was established among the Izi people in the 1970s by the Netherlands Reformed Congregations.

The Izi people are related to the Ibos but they speak their own language. They are found in the extreme north of traditional Ibo territory, in the area around Abakaliki and Iboko. There are around one million Izi people.

The first serious attempt to bring the Gospel to the Izi people was done by Mr. P. Meier, a Wycliffe translator. He translated the New Testament into the Izi language although he never founded a church.

In 1974 the Netherlands Reformed Congregations began a mission work among the Izi people. Mr. J. Commelin and sister A. Herfst were the first two NRC missionaries to work among the Izi. Sister Herfst was a nurse, and she stayed for only three months. Mr. Commelin worked among the Izi from 1974 to 1978.

The work was begun in the southern part of Izi, but when Miss Herfst left Mr. Commelin moved to the town of Onuenyim Agbaja in the northern part of Izi territory. This happened in December 1974.

The mission work was blessed with rapid growth at the start. In 1975 the first grass-roof church was built in Onuenyim Agbaja. In the same year evangelization and reading lessons were started in the surrounding villages. In 1983 Miss C. Renes began to organize local women's meetings.

In April 1988 four congregations were organized. On May 23, 1988, these congregations registered themselves with the government and they took the name Nigeria Reformed Church.

The Nigeria Reformed Church shares many of the beliefs and principles of the Netherlands Reformed Congregations. They subscribe to the Belgic Confession, the Heidelberg Catechism and the Canons of Dort. They hold to the basic belief of separation from the world; at present they are trying to decide how to apply this principle to the Nigerian situation. In particular, issues like music and dancing at weddings and a Christian form of burial are being examined in the light of God's Word.

Study questions

1. Describe the role played by Africans in the evangelization of Calabar.
2. Who are King Eyo Honesty, Essien Ukpabio and Mary Slessor?
3. To what extent is the Qua Iboe church Reformed?
4. Who are Samuel Bill and David Ekong?
5. What is a basic principle of the Nigeria Reformed Church?

Chapter Eight

Reformed Churches in Northern Nigeria

It is natural that the first part of Nigeria to receive the Gospel was the part closest to the sea. Thus in the 1840s and thereafter various missions brought the Gospel to the south of Nigeria. However around 1900 there was a growing awareness of the strategic importance of the north of Nigeria. The years right after 1900 saw a number of missions enter the north.

Four Reformed churches now exist because of this mission activity. They are the Christian Reformed Church of Nigeria, the Reformed Church of Christ in Nigeria, the Nongo u Kristu u ken Sudan hen Tiv, and the Evangelical Reformed Church of Christ. This chapter will look at these four churches.

Before we proceed, we must say something about the Sudan United Mission (SUM), for the early history of these churches is directly connected with the SUM.

The Sudan United Mission was begun by Dr. Karl Kumm. Dr. Kumm was a German who lived in England. He spent a few months in London at Harley College, where he met and later married Dr. Guinness's daughter Lucy. Kumm was a man who had a vision for Christianity in Africa. As he saw Islam advancing south into Africa, he felt that there was a need to establish Christian churches throughout the area south of the Sahara desert called the Sudan.[3] So in 1901 he founded the Sudan Pioneer Mission, which in 1904 became the Sudan United Mission. In 1904 Kumm led the first party of four persons, himself included, to the north of Nigeria. They settled in the town of Wase.

Dr. Kumm realized that an operation of this size required the cooperation of Christians from many different countries. So while the original branch of the SUM was British, Kumm traveled to other countries urging the foundation of national branches. In 1906 the American branch of the SUM was founded by the Evangelical Church (later the Evangelical United Brethren Church); it eventually worked in the Muri area. In the same year the South African branch was formed; it eventually worked both with the Tiv people and in the Mada Hills. In 1912 the Danish branch was founded, which came to Numan. In 1940 the Christian Reformed branch was formed after the death in 1933 of Johanna Veenstra, who had worked with the British branch in Takum. In addition there were New Zealand, Australian, Norwegian, Canadian, French and Swiss branches, all working in other African countries across the Sudan.

It goes without saying that not all of these branches were Reformed. Although Dr. Kumm was evangelical, he was not of Reformed persuasion. Our attention in the next pages will be on those churches that are specifically Reformed.

---

[3] "Sudan" has two meanings. It can refer to the country of Sudan. It can also refer to the mostly savanna land that lies between the Sahara Desert and the rain forest. The Sudan lies approximately between the latitudes of 8 and 16 degrees. It stretches 3500 miles across Africa from the Atlantic Ocean to the Red Sea. (See *Encyclopaedia Britannica*, under "Sudan.")

Christian Reformed Church of Nigeria

The present area of the CRCN first received the Gospel from members of the British branch of the SUM, who for the most part were not Reformed. In 1906, due to the lack of success in Wase, J.L. Maxwell, who was Presbyterian, and John Young opened a second SUM station, located in Wukari. Maxwell began studying the Jukun language. In 1907 the Donga station was opened by Messrs. Guinter, Hoover, Derr and Maxwell. 1908 saw the opening of the Ibi station. In 1911 Istifanus Lar, a Jukun, was baptized. In 1915 a Training Institute was opened in Wukari, but it was closed three years later. The first SUM church was constituted in Donga in 1917. By the end of 1922 there were organized churches in Donga, Wukari, and Ibi, as well as in Numan and Langtang.

The town of Takum was to become an important center for the Reformed witness. The SUM missionaries had been visiting Takum and the surrounding area, preaching the Gospel. In 1916 a young Christian from Donga, Timon Mama, settled in Takum as an evangelist. He was followed by Habu Likita and Filibbus Ashu, who also were evangelists. In 1919 a mission station was founded in Lupwe, outside of Takum, by William Bristow.

In 1920 Istifanus Audu was won to the Lord through the work of Habu Likita. He was baptized on April 6, 1922. He later became the first pastor in the Ekas Benue or CRCN church. Istifanus Audu joined the others in the work in the Takum area. Jonathan Wamada was baptized on the same day as Istifanus Audu, and he too assisted in the work in the Takum area.

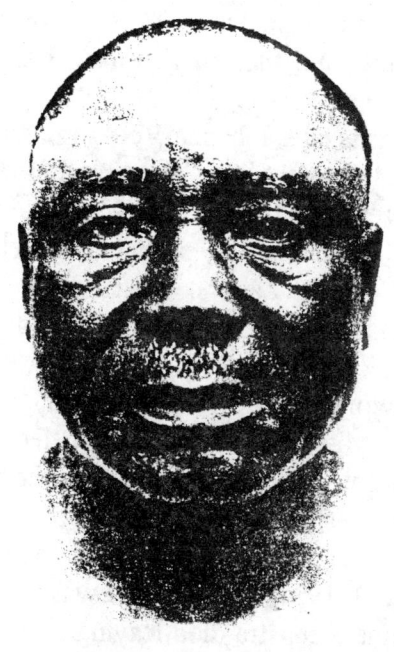

Pastor Istifanus Audu

It was during these years that Johanna Veenstra came to Lupwe. Johanna was born on April 19, 1894, in the city of Paterson, New Jersey, USA. Her father was a pastor in the Christian Reformed Church (CRC); he died when she was only eight years old. In 1913, feeling a call to serve the Lord in a special way, she enrolled in the Union Missionary Training Institute in New York, where she spent three years. The crucial moment in her life came in the summer of 1915 when she heard Karl Kumm speak at Lake Geneva in Wisconsin. Kumm presented the needs of Africa, and after three days of prayer, Johanna yielded to the call to come to Nigeria, but because she was only 21 she had to wait four years before she could go. Finally, in 1919 she sailed from New York, arriving in England, and at the end of the year she sailed for Nigeria, arriving in Lagos in January 1920. Johanna spent most of 1920 in Donga, and then in February 1921 she moved to Lupwe.

Two years later Johanna Veenstra assumed leadership of the work in Lupwe. She was engaged primarily in medical work and in preaching. In the following years she was joined by other CRC missionaries, particularly Nelle Breen, Jenny Stielstra and Bertha Zagers. Johanna Veenstra was also important in making the Christian Reformed Church in North America aware of the needs of Nigeria.

The work in Lupwe progressed gradually. But in March 1933, Miss Veenstra began to feel ill at a mission conference in Ibi. After the conference she traveled to Vom hospital where she had successful surgery. But soon thereafter she began to take a turn for the worse. On Palm Sunday, April 9, 1933, she died and was buried in Vom.

Johanna Veenstra died leaving a legacy. Because of her contacts and pleas with the Christian Reformed Church in North America, the CRC Synod of 1939 decided that it was ready to commit itself to working in Nigeria by taking over the responsibility of the Takum-Lupwe field from the British SUM. This occurred in January 1940. Later the CRC assumed responsibility for the present CRCN area.

In 1947 the CRC began to work in Wukari; in the same year they opened a new station in Baissa, with Rev. Harry Boer and then Rev Robert Recker as the first missionaries in Baissa. In the same year Mr. Istifanus Audu was ordained as the first Nigerian pastor of the CRC church.

July 25, 1951 is considered the organizational beginning of the EKAS Benue church, for then the original congregations of the Benue province decided to form their first Regional Church Council. In 1954 these churches ratified the 1951 decision, and they confirmed that the name of the church was Ekklesiyar Kristi a Sudan Lardin Benue (Church of Christ in the Sudan, Classis Benue), or EKAS Benue. In 1977 the Ekas Benue church changed its name to Christian Reformed Church of Nigeria (CRCN).

God has blessed the CRCN. At present there are more than 70 congregations with about 500 worship centers. The CRCN is working with a number of unreached tribes, and its evangelism program is very significant for the growth of the church in Nigeria. The CRCN seminary, Veenstra Seminary, is named after Johanna Veenstra and is located in Donga; the Smith Memorial Bible College in Baissa is named after the veteran missionary, Edgar Smith.

Reformed Church of Christ in Nigeria

The Kuteb people live in and near Takum. They were the people with whom Johanna Veenstra worked for most of her life in Nigeria. They were part of Ekas Benue or CRCN church until 1973. They thus share much of the history of the CRCN.

Unfortunately, due primarily to tribal differences, the majority of the Kutebs decided to leave the CRCN. This occurred in 1973. On November 5 of that year the Kuteb church became independent, calling itself Ekklesiyar Kristi a Nigeria, Lardin Takum (Church of Christ in Nigeria, Classis Takum). The abbreviated name was EKAN Takum.

On April 30, 1993, the church changed its name to Reformed Church of Christ in Nigeria (RCCN). This name is

Johanna Veenstra

a better expression of its national vision, Christian belief and doctrine, and Reformed persuasion and tradition.

A translation of the New Testament into the Kuteb language was done by Dr. "Andeyati" Rob Koops. This translation has been recently revised.

The RCCN is a church of mostly one ethnic group. It therefore has a special responsibility to bring the Gospel to the Kuteb people. However the evangelism activities of the

RCCN are not restricted to this people. Attempts are being made to reach people of other ethnic groups.

The RCCN has been blessed with rapid church growth. In 1973 it had 3 classes and 5 pastors; in 1995 there were 8 classes, 41 pastors and 45 consistories, with hundreds of preaching centers. The theological school of the RCCN is Veenstra Bible College and Seminary, located outside of Takum at Lupwe.

Nongo u Kristu u ken Sudan hen Tiv (NKST)

The Tiv people are a major tribe in Nigeria. Originally located around the Benue River, today there are several million Tiv people in Nigeria. The Gospel came to the Tiv people because of the inspiration of Karl Kumm.

In 1907 Dr. Kumm was invited to come to South Africa to present the needs of Nigeria and the Sudan. There was great interest in his message, and two men felt the call to come to Nigeria: Mr. George Botha, a member of the Dutch Reformed Church, and Mr. V.H. Hosking, a Wesleyan. In 1908 they went to England to prepare for their work in Nigeria. At the end of this year they traveled with Dr. Kumm to Nigeria.

Their original intention was to work with the Tiv people, but when they arrived in England they discovered that the American (Evangelical Church) branch of the SUM was working in Wukari and had responsibility for the Tiv field. So in 1909 Hosking, Botha and Carl Zimmerman began work up the Benue River among the Mbula people. But the Mbula people numbered only 8,000 people and there was a strong

Pastor J.E.I. Sai

Muslim influence there. The SUM then decided that it would be better for the missionaries to work among the Tiv people.

The work among the Tiv began in the village of Sai (or Saai or Salatu), 23 miles south of Wukari. At the beginning of 1911 Mr. Guinter and Rev. Botha came to explore the possibilities of work there. The people of Sai agreed, so on

April 17, 1911, Mr. Carl Zimmerman arrived in Sai and spent his first night in the compound of Mr. Sai, the head of the village. The next day he began constructing his house with Hausa-speaking workmen. Later, Mr. Hosking and Mr. Judd joined him.

The family of Mr. Sai were to be decisive in the beginnings of the Tiv church. On January 12, 1912, one of his sons, Akiga Sai, declared Christ to be his Savior. Another of his sons, J.E.I. Sai, was to be one of the first ordained pastors of the Tiv church, becoming an important leader of the church.

The South African branch of the SUM was comprised of missionaries of the Dutch Reformed Church, who were Afrikaans-speaking, and non-DRC missionaries, who were English-speaking. At first both groups of missionaries were working with the Tiv. Soon however the Dutch Reformed Church felt that it would be better to separate. This separation was finalized on July 1, 1916. At the end of 1915, Judd, Hosking and others started a work in Keana. The Dutch Reformed Church Mission (DRCM) continued to work among the Tiv.

Between 1913 and 1935 seven new mission stations were opened, including the station of Mkar, which was opened in 1923 and which became the center of the DRCM work. In 1926 the station of Sai was closed.

In these first years the growth of the church was slow. In the first 25 years of work, or by 1936, there were not more than 25 baptized Christians.[4] However, five years later there were already 214 of them. After 1936 the church began to grow rapidly. A significant reason for this growth is the establishment of village Bible schools throughout Tivland.

---

[4] E. Rubingh, *Sons of Tiv*, p. 123; E. Smith, *Nigerian Harvest*, p. 277.

These rural Bible schools became a powerful indigenous tool for the spread of the Gospel.

In the 1930s and 1940s the DRCM opened many primary schools. These schools have also been a powerful impetus to the growth of the church in Tivland.

The translation of the Bible into the Tiv language was vital for the success of this new church. In 1914 Mr. Judd published the first booklet in the Tiv language. The first Gospel in Tiv was published in 1916, and the whole New Testament was completed in 1936. Rev. Orffer wrote the first draft of the Old Testament between 1938 and 1951; his translation was reviewed and completed on 1961.

January 9, 1957 is the birthdate of the autonomous Tiv church, the Nongo u Kristu u ken Sudan hen Tiv (NKST). At that time the NKST had about 1800 baptized members and about 23,000 people attending services every Sunday.

During the 1950s the South African DRCM began to realize that its resources were being overextended and that there was also mission work to be done closer to South Africa. In addition, political developments at home made the South Africans less welcome in Nigeria. So during the 1950s and finally by November 1961 the mission work of the DRCM was handed over to the Christian Reformed Church, which shared the same Reformed confession as the DRCM and NKST.

At present, by the grace of God, the NKST is a strong church, fully conscious of its Reformed heritage. They have at least 200 congregations and many preaching centers. Their seminary is the Reformed Theological College of Nigeria, located in Mkar; the Benue Bible Institute is located in Harga. The Hilltop University in Mkar is a recent attempt to establish a Christian university in Nigeria.

Evangelical Reformed Church of Christ

The early history of the ERCC and the NKST are closely related because both churches originally proceeded out of the work of the South African branch of the SUM. We have seen how Dr. Kumm came to South Africa in 1907 to arouse interest in the work in Nigeria. One of the two men who first responded to the call of Dr. Kumm was Mr. Vincent H. Hosking. In 1908 he came with Rev. Botha to Nigeria. In the next year they began the work among the Mbula people, but this work was closed down after two years. In 1911 Mr. Hosking went to Sai, and the next year Mr. Judd joined him there.

We have seen that the South African mission eventually decided to separate into two fields: the Afrikaans-speaking DRCM worked with the Tiv, while the English-speaking non-DRCM missionaries decided to go north of the Benue River. In February 1915 Mr. Judd crossed the Benue looking for a place for the English-speaking South African missionaries to work. He had hoped to start a work among the Mada people, but since there was no suitable opportunity, he decided to begin work in the town of Keana among the Alago people. On July 1, 1916 the South African branch of the SUM handed the work among the Tiv to the DRCM and they opened a new field north of the Benue River. Mr. Judd and Mr. Hosking went to Keana to begin this new work.

In 1917 new workers from South Africa joined the missionaries in Keana. In the same year, Mr. Hosking died of yellow fever and was buried in Keana. During this time Mr. and Mrs. Judd began to translate the Gospel of Mark into the Alago language.

A few years later, in 1920, Mr. Judd, the leader of the mission, opened a station in the town of Randa. Randa became the headquarters of the mission for many years. In that same year a school for Christian Religious Instruction (C.R.I.) was established in Randa. Pastor Mamma Audu and Pastor Ambi were two of the notable products of this school. In December 1922 the Lord's Supper was celebrated at Randa for the first time, with three members partaking.

In March 1924 the missionaries in Randa spent a week of prayer and fasting to determine where they should open a new work. After this week Rev. Ivan Hepburn and Mr. J. Dawson visited Lezzin Lafia, which is now Wana. In 1926 Rev. Hepburn moved to Wana, and began work there.

Other stations were opened in Lafia in 1932, Ancho in 1937, Wamba in 1939, and later in Alushi, Kagbu, Obi and Ayu. By God's grace, the number of believers and churches grew so that by 1957 there were 171 places of worship in this church area.

The Women's Fellowship of the future ERCC had its origins in the work of Miss Anne Beaumont and Miss E.R. Rimmer. 1942 is considered the beginnings of this important wing of the church.

The 1950s was the time when the church became autonomous. In May 1956 this church was registered with the government as Ekklesiyar Krista a Sudan, Lardin Dutsen Mada, which is Hausa for EKAS Mada Hills.

1958 was another joyful year, for the first two ordinations of this new church took place. In January 16 Pastor Ambi was ordained in Randa; two days later Pastor Abimiku Anzaku was ordained in Keffin Wambai.

In 1959 a Bible School was opened in Murya, and in 1964 the Ayu Bible Institute was founded, which later became the Ayu Theological Seminary.

The 1960s were a time of readjustment, when because of political reasons the South African missionaries had to leave Nigeria. The Mada Hills church experienced both the difficulties and rewards of being completely autonomous.

The Mada Hills church later changed its name to Church of Christ in Central Nigeria (CCCN); around 1990 the church became Reformed and adopted the name Evangelical Reformed Church of Christ (ERCC). Since the church still practices only adult baptism, we could refer to them as a Reformed Baptist church.

ERCC has a strategic location in Nigeria, being located in the center of the country. God has blessed the church with growth, and it is has an important place in the churches in the north of the country.

Study questions

1. What was the reason for the establishing of the Sudan United Mission? Who founded the SUM?
2. Describe the significance of Johanna Veenstra for the CRCN and the RCCN.
3. How is the ethnic situation of the NKST and the RCCN similar? What special advantages and problems do they have?
4. Contrast the effects of the departure of the South African missionaries on the NKST and the ERCC.
5. How is the theology of the ERCC similar to that of Charles Spurgeon? (See the end of Chapter 3.)

Chapter Nine

Reformed Ecumenical Fellowships

The Reformed and Presbyterian churches in Nigeria have realized the need to have fellowship with each other and also with other Christians in the country. In this chapter we will look at two Nigerian ecumenical organizations and three Reformed organizations that some of our churches have joined.

Most of the Nigerian churches that we have looked at are members of the Christian Association of Nigeria (CAN). CAN is an inter-denominational association that has become an important political organization since the 1980s because of Muslim opposition. CAN has often spoken out in defense of Christian rights. Both Catholics and Protestant churches are members of CAN. CAN is an expression of Christian unity in Nigeria.

In the north of Nigeria, there is the Tarrayar Ekklesiyoyin Kristi a Nigeria (TEKAN), or, the Fellowship of the Churches of Christ in Nigeria. TEKAN is the community of churches that arose out of the work of the Sudan United Mission.

The decision to form TEKAN was made in Langtang in 1954, fifty years after Karl Kumm and his party first arrived in Wase. The organization was then called TEKAS. Today, the CRCN, NKST, ERCC and NRC are the Reformed members of TEKAN. RCCN is applying for membership.

TEKAN helps give unity to the Christians in the north of Nigeria. TEKAN is the proprietor of the Theological College of Northern Nigeria (TCNN), located in Bukuru.

World Alliance of Reformed Churches

An international Reformed organization to which some of our churches belong is the World Alliance of Reformed Churches (WARC). WARC is a large ecumenical organization closely related to the World Council of Churches. It has about 200 member churches throughout the world. About fifty of these church denominations are African.

WARC is an old ecumenical organization, founded in 1877. Originally it was called the World Presbyterian Alliance. WARC tends to focus on ethical issues instead of doctrinal ones.

In the 1980s the South African theologian, Allan Boesak, was the president of WARC. Boesak is a Reformed pastor and also a black liberation theologian. Many of the theological statements of WARC are concerned with social and political issues. WARC is strongly sympathetic to liberation theology.

The PCN, ERCC and RCCN are members of WARC.

Reformed Ecumenical Council

The Reformed Ecumenical Council (REC) is a smaller organization than WARC, although its member churches have between 5 and 6 million members. The REC was originally known as the Reformed Ecumenical Synod (RES); in 1988 it changed its name to REC.

The REC was founded in 1946 by three conservative Reformed churches of Dutch background: the Christian Reformed Church in North America, the Reformed Churches in the Netherlands, and the Reformed Churches in South Africa (NGK). The REC emphasizes the authority of the Bible, the importance of the traditional Reformed and Presbyterian confessions, and the vision of the Kingdom of God. Its members tend to be more conservative in their theology.

At present the REC has 29 member church denominations which are found in 20 countries throughout the world. In Africa, there are member churches in Botswana, Malawi, Namibia, South Africa, Zambia, Zimbabwe, as well as in Nigeria. The CRCN and the NKST are member churches; the RCCN has provisional membership. Representatives of the member churches of the REC meet once every four years in a general council.

The Reformed Ecumenical Council of Nigeria

In June 1991, after meetings in Geneva and Calabar, delegates from five Nigerian Reformed churches met at TCNN in Bukuru and agreed to form a Reformed fellowship in Nigeria. These five churches were the PCN, NKST, CRCN, ERCC and the RCCN. A committee was formed to draw up a constitution, and the constitution was approved on May 29, 1992. The name Reformed Ecumenical Council of Nigeria (RECON) was chosen. Because the council was founded at the time of persecution, the motto "Burning, yet not consumed" was chosen. The reference of the motto is to the burning bush of Moses. This bush together with a cross on a map of Nigeria forms the logo. At the time of this writing RECON is still young but it has the potential of making a significant Reformed witness in Nigeria.

In the mid 1990s, HEKAN Kaduna, or the United Church in Kaduna, joined RECON. HEKAN Kaduna is a church composed of members of the various TEKAN churches who live in the Kaduna area.

Conclusion

We have now come to the end of our historical survey. We have walked a long road, starting in Geneva in the sixteenth century and arriving in Nigeria at the end of the twentieth century. We have seen how the ideas of John Calvin about the lordship of God have influenced many Christians in many different times and places. Many churches call themselves Presbyterian or Reformed because of the influence of Calvin's theology. Through God's providence, Reformed and Presbyterian churches can be found in many places throughout the world. In the next chapters we will consider some of the basic ideas of the Reformed faith.

Study questions

1. Name three Nigerian ecumenical organizations. Which ones are Reformed?
2. What are the main differences between the WARC and the REC?
3. What are the differences between the REC and the RECON?
4. To which ecumenical organizations does your church belong?

PART TWO.

REFORMED AND PRESBYTERIAN BELIEFS

Chapter Ten

The Reformed Worldview: The Lordship of God

The above pages traced the history of the Reformed movement from John Calvin up to present-day Nigeria. The question that now must be asked is: What do these Reformed and Presbyterian churches believe? What are some of the basic beliefs that are common to the churches that we have surveyed in the above pages?

The Reformed movement is now about 450 years old, with churches in many different countries. Obviously these churches are not exactly the same in every matter of belief and practice. The Reformed church in Geneva at the time of John Calvin was not the same as John Knox's Scottish Presbyterian church; the Presbyterian church in Scotland today is not the same as the Presbyterian church in Nigeria.

The Reformed faith has been adapted to different cultures and situations in different periods of time. There has been some contextualization or inculturation of the Reformed faith over the course of history.

An obvious example of this contextualization is liturgy and music. In some of the early Reformed and Presbyterian churches, there were no musical instruments in the church. Gradually in many of the Reformed churches in Europe, the organ became the only instrument used. Today, in Nigeria, African instruments are increasingly being used, and the liturgy is being adapted to the African culture.

Another example is that of polygamy. Because polygamy was not a problem at the time of Calvin, he said very little about it. But the Reformed and Presbyterian churches in Nigeria have done significant thinking about this issue. They have taken positions that they believe are faithful to Scripture and relevant to their culture.

However, although there are differences among the various Reformed churches, there is also a common heritage. The Reformed and Presbyterian churches throughout the centuries and throughout the world have held to common beliefs and practices. We want to consider some of these beliefs here.

The first thing that should be said about the Reformed faith is that it holds to most of the beliefs of the early church. The Reformed and Presbyterian churches believe the basic Christian teachings that are found in the Apostles' Creed and which are held by Christians throughout the world. Our churches hold to the decisions of the Council of Nicea (AD 325), which said that the Son is of the same essence as the Father; we accept the Council of Chalcedon (AD 451), which said that Jesus is one person with two natures (the divine and human natures).

Our churches accept the classic Christian doctrine of the Trinity. We believe in the vicarious atonement of Christ and all other basic Christian doctrines. So the Reformed and

Presbyterian churches stand in the mainstream of Christian orthodoxy.

Secondly, it should be said that the Reformed and Presbyterian churches are part of the Protestant movement. The Protestant churches are those churches that came out of the sixteenth-century Reformation. Reformed theology is close to Lutheran, Anglican and Baptist theology. The Reformed and Presbyterian churches agree with other Protestant churches on most points of doctrine. The points of unity are many; the differences are relatively few.

Nevertheless, there are obviously some special teachings and emphases that characterize our churches. We want to look at some of these aspects now.

The Reformed Worldview: The Lordship of God

We will start by asking the question: What is the central idea of the Reformed and Presbyterian faith? Although different answers have been given, there is general agreement that the kingship or lordship of God and of Christ is the basic characteristic of our faith.[5] The Reformed faith has a strong awareness that God is King over the entire world and over all of our lives. Therefore, our lives must be lived in reverence before God.

Calvin's *Institutes* are full of this emphasis on the glory and majesty of God. In the first pages Calvin talks of the awe that believers feel when they are before the presence of God. He says that man cannot become aware of his lowly state "until he has compared himself with God's majesty." He then

---

[5] Although many theologians talk of the sovereignty of God, we think that the lordship or kingship of God is a better expression of the personal rule and majesty of God.

quotes Isaiah 24:23, which says that "the sun will blush and the moon be confounded when the Lord of Hosts shall reign."[6]

We believe that this theme of the lordship of God and of Christ is a key to understanding all of Reformed theology. In the following pages we will look at Reformed and Presbyterian theology from this perspective.

If God is indeed a true King, then it is clear that his kingship is over all of our lives. God is King both in our church services and also in the rest of our lives. He is King both on Sundays and also in the rest of the week. The Reformed people believe strongly that God is King over all of our lives. We believe that all of life is religion.

The Reformed and Presbyterian faith is thus not just a collection of doctrines about salvation. Instead, the Reformed faith is a Christian perspective on all of life.

We thus call Calvinism a *worldview* (or a world-and-life view). It is a Christian perspective on all of the world and on all of life. Professor Albert Wolters defines a worldview as "the comprehensive framework of one's basic beliefs about things."[7] In other words, a worldview is a way of viewing all of reality.

There are different possible worldviews. A Marxist worldview sees everything from the perspective of economic oppression and liberation. All of reality is then interpreted from economic, communistic principles.

A humanistic worldview sees everything from the perspective of the glory of man. Humanism looks at history, government and the family in order to glorify man.

---

[6] *Institutes* I.1.3 (Book I, Chapter 1, Section 3); pp. 38-39. (All quotations from the *Institutes* are taken from the translation by Ford Lewis Battles. See bibliography.)

[7] Albert Wolters, *Creation Regained* (Grand Rapids, 1985), p. 2.

Islam is also a worldview. The Muslims are very clear that the Koran relates to all of life. The Muslims want to make Nigeria, for example, a Muslim country in every aspect. Islam believes that all of life is religion.

Traditional African religion is a worldview. This religion believes that the Supreme God and the divinities affect all of life. If you want a good farm, you have to honor the gods. If you want children, you have to sacrifice to the gods. Traditional African religion believes that all of life is religion.

Unfortunately, many of the early missionaries to Africa did not see Christianity as a comprehensive worldview. They taught the first converts that they should not get involved in politics because they said politics were not Christian. So the Christians ran away from politics and left the government to the Muslims!

But the Reformed faith in its truest sense is a worldview, affecting all of life. The Reformed faith believes that since Christ is King over all of life, all of life should be brought under his lordship.

The Kingdom of God

Let us now look at the basic elements of the Reformed worldview. This worldview is very simple and very profound. It believes in the creation, fall and redemption of all aspects of the world.

The doctrine of creation reminds us that the whole of the world belongs to God. All of life is subject to God because he made it all. The doctrine of creation tells us that this world was originally good. Man was created in a perfect relationship with God, his neighbor and the world. Adam and Eve had fellowship with God in the garden. They lived in harmony with God and with each other. There was no sin at that time. Our first parents cared for the earth, having been given dominion over the world.

When sin came, it too was universal in its effect. Sin affected all of creation. The relationship of Adam and Eve with God was ruined, and they hid from God because they were afraid. They began to accuse each other for the sin they had committed. Sin also affected the physical world. Thorns appeared in the fields, work for man became tedious, and the woman experienced pain in childbirth.

The Reformed idea of redemption embraces all aspects of creation. Not just our souls are redeemed. All of creation is being redeemed through Jesus Christ. All of these broken relationships are being restored through Christ. Of course, the perfect redemption of creation will occur when Jesus comes again.

We believe that the term "Kingdom of God" describes this restoration of all of creation. The Kingdom of God is the reign of God and our obedience to this reign. Wherever God's reign is acknowledged, there the Kingdom of God is. Wherever people obey God, there life will be transformed and renewed.

For example, sin brought disharmony in marriage relationships. But where Christ reigns, love and harmony will prevail. Again, sinful behavior has brought destruction and erosion to our farms and land. But where Christ reigns and where people care for the earth, some of these problems will be made less. Sin has also affected our political life. Injustice and corruption are very common in government. But where Christ reigns, justice and honesty will prevail. In the market we see the effects of sin. Cheating and dishonesty are common in the marketplace. But where Christ reigns, honesty and fair dealing will be found. In our churches we see pride and tribalism. But where Christ reigns, there will be humility and brotherly love. In our society people suffer from the power of evil spirits. But where Christ reigns, Satan and his demons will be cast out.

I think you can see how the Kingdom of God affects all of life. The Kingdom of God can be seen in the market, in the school, in the home, in the government and in the church.

In our world there is spiritual warfare between two kingdoms: the Kingdom of God and the kingdom of Satan. The kingdom of Satan is present wherever there is hatred, pride, corruption, dishonesty, immorality or idolatry. The Kingdom of God is present wherever God's name is honored in any sphere or area of life.

The King of the Kingdom

The king in this Kingdom is obviously God himself. The Old Testament speaks often of the reign of God over the whole earth. Psalms 93, 95, 97 and 99 talk of the universal reign of God. But although God reigned over the whole earth in the Old Testament times, only a few people in the small country of Israel submitted to his reign. The universal reign of God is the Kingdom of God in the general or broader sense.

The reign of God in the special sense is seen when lives are brought into obedience to God. The Kingdom of God in this special sense was present in the history of Israel in the Old Testament in just a small way. But the Gospels tell us that the Kingdom of God came in a special and bigger way when Jesus began his ministry. John the Baptist preached: "Repent for the kingdom of heaven is near" (Matt. 3:2; cf. Matt. 4:17). Luke 16:16 suggests that the Old Testament age was the age of the Law and the Prophets, and the New Testament age is that of the Kingdom of God.

The special sense of the Kingdom of God is fully evident in the reign of Jesus. This dimension of the Kingdom is present whenever Jesus reigns and whenever people obey this reign. This second usage is that which is common in the New Testament.

The New Testament teaches that Jesus is now reigning for the Father. The reign of Jesus began after his resurrection and ascension. After Jesus rose from the dead, he ascended into heaven and sat at the right hand of the Father. We confess this in the Apostles' Creed when we say that Jesus "ascended into heaven and sits at the right hand of God the Father." We also find this teaching in Ephesians 1:20-22, where Paul says that God raised Christ from the dead "and seated him at his right hand in the heavenly realms far above all rule and authority... And God placed all things under his feet and appointed him to be head over everything for the church." The words "to sit at his right hand" refer to the special power and authority that the Father has given the Son.

It is clear from Scripture that Jesus is now reigning in heaven for his Father. He is the Father's deputy governor, so to speak. (Calvin calls Christ "the lieutenant of God.") Paul teaches this in 1 Corinthians 15:25 where he says that "Christ must reign until he has put all his enemies under his feet." Then, at the end, Christ will hand back the kingdom to the Father (vs. 24). Christ is now ruling so that his Kingdom might be brought to completion. When his Kingdom is completed, then God the Trinity will rule in eternity (see vs. 28).

The Scepter of the King: Scripture

If Christ is our King, how does he reign? Calvin uses colorful language when he calls the Word of God the scepter of

Christ.[8] The idea is that the scepter of a king is his rod of authority by which things happen. In Esther 5:2, the king held out his gold scepter to Esther, which gave her permission to come to him. So, in a similar way, Jesus Christ rules the world and his church through his Word, which is his instrument of authority.

Calvin believed in the power of Scripture, which he believed was the Word of God. The Word of God, together with the Holy Spirit, will bring repentance.

The Reformed and Presbyterian churches have always had a high regard for the authority of Scripture. This belief came from the Reformation. At the time of the Reformation, the Roman Catholic Church often did not want their people to read the Bible. For example, a church council in Toulouse in France in 1229 said that the people should not read the Bible. The church in England during the time of John Wyclif discouraged the people from reading the Bible. The Roman Catholic Church said that there were *two* sources of theology: the Bible *and* church tradition.

Against this, Martin Luther and John Calvin taught *sola Scriptura* (only Scripture). Scripture is the Word of God through which God speaks to us. Scripture is therefore the only authority in our theology and in our life. The Bible is the rule for doctrine and life. Our theology must be Biblical.

Reformed theology tries to be fully Biblical. We try to speak where the Bible speaks; we try to be silent where the Bible is silent. We try to take *all* of Scripture seriously.

It is easy when reading the Bible to skip over a passage that we do not like or do not understand. Some people do not like the teaching of election, so when they come to those parts

---

[88] See Calvin's commentaries on Ps. 2:9; Ps. 45:6-7; Ps. 110:2; Ps. 149:9; Is. 2:4; Hos. 1:11; Mic. 4:3, and other passages.

of the Bible, they pass over them. But the Reformed and Presbyterian tradition tries to take every part of the Bible seriously for it is all the Word of God. The great Reformed Baptist, Charles Spurgeon, said that a good theologian will never blink or shut his eyes when reading the Bible.

Of course the Bible has to be properly interpreted. When Jesus said that Herod was a fox (Luke 13:32), he did not mean that Herod was an animal with four legs and a tail. Jesus was using a metaphor to show that Herod was a wicked person. Historical passages in the Bible should be read as history; parables as parables; metaphors as metaphors; and prophecy as prophecy.

The Reformed and Presbyterians believe that since all of Scripture is God's Word, there will not be theological errors or contradictions in the Bible. There will be different emphases and different theologies, but not contradicting theologies. Paul will emphasize faith and James will teach works, but Paul does not contradict James. They are each teaching two sides of one faith.

The belief in the authority of Scripture is a basic starting point for Reformed theology. It is a basic Reformed principle about method, about how to do theology.

It is clear from this chapter that the lordship of God is the most important idea of Reformed theology. The next chapters will see how this idea is found in the doctrines of election, providence, sanctification, the church and eschatology.

Study Questions

1. What is the central idea of Reformed theology?
2. What is a worldview? Give three examples of worldviews.

3. What is the Reformed worldview?
4. Why is the doctrine of creation important to our life in Nigeria today?
5. How is the Reformed worldview relevant to traders in the market? To teachers in the primary school? To state governors? To parents at home?
6. When does Jesus Christ reign?
7. What is the difference between the Roman Catholic and Reformed views of Scripture?

Chapter Eleven

God's Lordship in Conversion: Election

When people talk of Calvinism, they usually think of election and predestination. We hope that the previous section on the Reformed worldview has shown that Calvinism is far more than these two doctrines. Although the Five Points of Calvinism talk of salvation in its narrow sense, the Reformed perspective deals with the lordship of Christ over all of life.

Nonetheless, it is true that Calvinism does talk of election. The reason we talk of election is that the Bible talks of election. So we should speak where the Bible speaks and be silent where the Bible is silent.

Election

It should be said first that one cannot fully understand election. This is because election is something that happens in the mind of God, which we cannot fully understand. We should remember that God is infinite and we are finite, so we cannot comprehend everything that God does. We should realize that we are not God.

So what does Scripture say about election? Before we go on, let us define election. "To elect" means to choose; "election" then means choosing. In Nigeria we have elections when the people elect or choose political leaders. The people elect or choose a candidate; the process of choosing is called an election.

The Bible teaches us that God elects or chooses various nations or people in different times and places. In Genesis 1-11 we see how the people that God made disobeyed him repeatedly. So God chose one man, Abraham, and his family to be his people so that the Messiah would come from his family to save mankind. This is election, the choosing of Abraham and his family. Why did God choose Abraham and not someone else? We don't know, but we do know that he did it for our good and salvation.

During the time of the Egyptian bondage, God renewed his choice of Abraham's children, who were then the people of Israel. Deuteronomy 7:6 says that God chose or elected the people of Israel out of all the nations of the earth to be his people, his treasured possession. Why did God choose Israel instead of Assyria or Egypt? We don't know. But we know that God did it for his own good reasons.

Did God choose the Israelites because they were many? No! Deuteronomy 7:7 says that they were the fewest of all peoples. Did God choose them because they were good? No! Deuteronomy 9:6 says that they were a stiff-necked people. Instead, God chose them out of his love and for his good purposes. These passages teach the election of Israel. (You should read and study Deuteronomy 7:6-9 and 9:4-6 for their lessons on election.)

Many people fail to see the beauty of the doctrine of election. Election teaches us that we were sinful and spiritually dead and that God out of his love rescued us from our sin and misery. Election is a doctrine that talks of God's love.

Ezekiel 16 is a beautiful story about how God elected and saved Israel. In this chapter God compares Israel (or Jerusalem) to a new-born baby girl that was found abandoned in a field (vss. 4-5). The baby was dirty and covered with blood. God found that baby, he washed her, cared for her, gave her good clothes, and soon that baby girl grew up into a beautiful woman. Eventually God entered into a covenant with her and married her (vs. 8). This is election! God loved Israel and chose her when she was hopeless and helpless, and he gave her a good life. This is the grace of God which is still reaching out to the hopeless and helpless.

The first three chapters of Hosea talk of election in a similar way. There was a very bad prostitute called Gomer. (She represents Israel.) God told Hosea to take Gomer for his wife and show her love. Hosea did this and rescued Gomer out of her sinfulness. This again is an example of election! God chose Israel when she was very bad. He did this purely out of love.

However, in Ezekiel 16 and Hosea 2, the woman leaves her husband and becomes a prostitute again. This is a picture of Israel, who left God. But in Hosea 3, God told Hosea to find Gomer again and buy her back and bring her home. Hosea again showed his love to Gomer and bought her back.

These stories show the sovereign love of God toward Israel. God loved and chose Israel. They also show the fact that Israel had a responsibility to be faithful to God.

The Reformed faith talks of divine sovereignty and human responsibility in relation to election. Divine sovereignty refers to God's power in doing what he wants to do. God saves those whom he wants to save. Human responsibility means that we human beings are responsible for our behavior. A person is responsible to accept Jesus Christ as his Savior. Somehow both divine sovereignty and human responsibility are true. Our salvation rests in God's hands, but we are responsible for our faith or lack of faith.

The Old Testament talks especially of the election or choosing of Israel; the New Testament talks of the election of the church and of individual Christians. The teaching of election is found in many parts of the New Testament and should be taken seriously.

Ephesians 1:4-5 says that God "chose us in [Christ] before the creation of the world to be holy and blameless in his sight. In his love he predestined us to be adopted." Ephesians 1:11 says that in Christ "we were also chosen, having been predestined according to the plan" of God. This is a clear teaching of Paul on election.

Romans 8:29-30 says that those whom God knew (or loved) beforehand, he "predestined to be conformed to the likeness of his Son ... and those he predestined he called." Romans 9 wrestles with the problem of why God chose Jacob and not Esau. But Paul says that God is not unjust for he will have mercy on whom he will have mercy, and he will have compassion on whom he will have compassion (vvs. 14-15). We don't know why God chose Jacob, but we know that he did so out of love.

Peter's first letter is written to "God's elect, strangers in the world ..., who have been chosen according to the foreknowledge of God the Father, by the sanctifying work of the Spirit" (1 Peter 1:1-2). Acts 13:48 talks of the Gentiles in Antioch of Pisidia who believed because they were "appointed for eternal life."

In 2 Thessalonians 2:13 Paul says that "from the beginning God chose you through the sanctifying work of the Spirit."

These and other texts teach that God has chosen some people "before the creation of the world" (Eph. 1:4) to be his children. They were chosen out of love to be saved.

Irresistible Grace

Closely related to the doctrine of election is the doctrine of irresistible grace. The doctrine of irresistible grace says that the special grace of the Holy Spirit enters those who are elect and causes them to become believers. This is logical, for if a person is elect, then someone has to bring this person to Christ. Scripture teaches that it is the Holy Spirit who brings a person to salvation.

In his talk with Nicodemus, Jesus says that a person will enter the Kingdom of God only if he is "born of water and the Spirit." (Water refers to baptism; the Spirit refers to the Holy Spirit.) Jesus continued: "Flesh gives birth to flesh, and the Spirit gives birth to spirit." Then Jesus describes how the Spirit works. The Spirit is like the wind that blows wherever it wants. "So it is with everyone born of the Spirit" (John 3:5-8).

This passage shows us that it is the Holy Spirit who causes a person to be born again. The Spirit blows where he wills. Obviously the Holy Spirit is causing those who had been chosen to become believers.

For this reason, Jesus could say: "All that the Father gives me will come to me." And: "No one can come to me unless the Father who sent me draws him" (John 6:37,44). The elect are those who are given to the Son by the Father; the Father will draw or pull the elect to the Son by the power of the Holy Spirit.

So, when Paul was in Philippi preaching the Gospel, there was a woman named Lydia who believed. How did she believe? Acts 16:14 says that "the Lord opened her heart to respond to Paul's message." How did God open her heart? Obviously, through the work of the Holy Spirit.

In our prayers many of us pray that God will change someone's heart. This is a prayer for the Spirit to come and to bring him or her to Christ. This is a belief in the saving power of the Holy Spirit. This is a Calvinistic prayer!

Total Depravity

If it is only the Holy Spirit who can bring a person to salvation, then this implies that an unbeliever's will is in bondage to sin and this person cannot choose for Christ on his own. This is the doctrine of total depravity. Total depravity says that an unbeliever's life is directed completely away from God and he cannot do anything good unless the Holy Spirit brings him to Christ.

Scripture confirms that total depravity is true. Paul in Ephesians says that the unbeliever was "dead in transgressions and sins" (Eph. 2:1). A dead man cannot believe unless the Spirit revives him.

John 6:44 says that no one can come to Christ unless the Father draws him. We are unable to come by ourselves; we will only come if God draws or pulls us. Romans 3:10-18 and Jeremiah 17:9 and other passages teach us how radical sin is in the non-Christian life.

Calvin was not the first person to talk of total depravity and irresistible grace. A thousand years before him, there was a young man in North Africa whose name was Augustine. Augustine's mother was Christian and his father was pagan. His mother, Monica, prayed without ceasing that her son would become a Christian. But Augustine lived a bad life and he ran away from the Gospel. Augustine resisted the Gospel. Finally the Holy Spirit spoke to him in a garden and changed his heart. Augustine later said that he was totally depraved, unable to believe, and it was only the grace of God's Spirit that changed his heart.

Martin Luther was another person who believed that the unbelieving person is sinful and unable to believe in Christ by himself. Luther was always aware of the power of God's grace which leads to faith.

During the Reformation, there was a very good man by the name of Erasmus. Erasmus thought that people generally are pretty good and that they can believe on their own. He believed in the freedom of the human will.

But Luther said that this belief of Erasmus undermines the grace of God. Luther said that a man's will is in bondage to Satan and only the Holy Spirit can free this will. In 1525 he wrote a book called *The Bondage of the Will*. In this book he taught the doctrines of election, total depravity and irresistible grace.

The Reformed believe in total depravity, but this applies only to a person before he believes. Obviously if a person believes in Christ, he is no longer totally depraved because the Spirit of God has transformed this person.

Perseverance of the Saints

If God has chosen someone and if it is the Holy Spirit who causes his salvation, then obviously the person will remain in the faith until he dies. This is the doctrine of the perseverance of the saints. Once a person is truly saved, he is always saved.

Of course, this doctrine applies only to those who are truly saved. Often a person will make a confession of faith that is not genuine. There are also some people who believe for a while and then backslide. But if the Holy Spirit has really worked in a person's heart in a saving way, then this person will be preserved until the end. (God preserves and therefore the person perseveres.)

To a certain extent, this doctrine is a tautology. In other words, it states the obvious. It simply says that the elect will really be saved. But this doctrine also has deep pastoral significance. It says that the Holy Spirit will guard and keep his own through all difficulties.

This doctrine is a reminder that we are "sealed with the promised Holy Spirit, who is a deposit guaranteeing our inheritance" until our redemption (Eph. 1:13-14). A seal guarantees that something will happen, and the Holy Spirit is our seal.

God will protect those who belong to him. "The Lord is faithful, and he will strengthen and protect you from the evil one" (2 Thess. 3:3). Believers are "shielded [or guarded] by God's power" until the last day (2 Peter 1:5). The reason for this security is that "he who began a good work in you will carry it on to completion until the day of Christ Jesus" (Phil. 1:6). That which God starts, he will finish.

We have the promise that Jesus "shall lose none of those whom the Father gave to him, but he will raise them up in the last day" (John 6:39). We believe that "neither death nor life, neither angels nor demons, neither the present nor the future, nor any powers ... will be able to separate us from the love of God that is in Christ Jesus our Lord" (Rom. 8:38-39). This is because of the preservation of God that results in the perseverance of the saints.

Limited Atonement

Total depravity, unconditional election, irresistible grace and the perserverance of the saints are four of the Five Points of Calvinism. All of them are directly related to the doctrine of election, which is clearly taught in Scripture. The other doctrine traditionally associated with election is limited atonement. Limited atonement is not clearly taught in Scripture but is a logical deduction from the idea of the atonement.

The doctrine of atonement says that Christ died on the cross to pay for our sins. Now obviously if one's sins are paid for, then the person is saved. It is also clear that not everyone is saved. So limited atonement says that Christ died to pay for the sins of only those who are elect and who believe in him.

There are passages in Scripture that seem to teach limited atonement. In John 10:11, Jesus says that the good shepherd lays down his life for his sheep. In verse 15 Jesus says that he is the good shepherd who lays down his life for his sheep. In other words, Christ died for his sheep or for his own.

Ephesians 5:25 says that "Christ loved the church and gave himself up for her."

In 2 Corinthians 5:14 Paul says that Christ "died for all, therefore all died." This verse seems to contradict limited atonement, for Paul says that Christ "died for all." But who are these "all"? The next phrase says that "all died." But who died? In Pauline theology, only the believers truly died with Christ. (See Romans 6:2-4.) So in this passage, the "all" refers to all of the believers who died with Christ, not all of the people in the world.

(We should remember that in the Bible "all" does not always mean "all" in a literal sense. When Mark 1:5 says that all the people of Judea and Jerusalem went to hear John the Baptist, this does not include every single individual. Obviously some lame and old people did not go; probably some children did not go; and of course the high priest likely did not go to hear John. When Acts 19:10 says that all of the people in Asia heard the Gospel, this again does not include every single individual. "All" in these passages is figurative language for "many" or "most.")

In John 1:29, John the Baptist talks of the Lamb of God that takes away the sin of the world. Again, one should ask, what does "sin of the world" mean? Probably it means the sin of people from all parts of the world, not necessarily the sin of every person in the world.

Christ died in an efficacious way to pay for the sins of the believers; but Christ's death is sufficient to pay for the sins of anyone who believes in him.

Five Points of Calvinism

The Synod of Dort taught the Five Points of Calvinism. (See chapter 5 above.) The Five Points of Calvinism are easily remembered by the word TULIP. TULIP stands for the first letters of total depravity, unconditional election, limited atonement, irresistible grace and perseverance of the saints. Obviously, election is the heart of the Five Points of Calvinism.

One should remember that we can never fully understand election. This is because we are human and finite. God's wisdom surpasses ours. One should think about God's words to Job at the end of that book. "Will the one who contends with the Almighty correct him? Let him who accuses God answer him!" (Job 40:2; see also Job 38 and 39.)

One should consider what Paul says about "the depth of the riches of the wisdom and knowledge of God. How unsearchable are his judgments, and his paths beyond tracing out. Who has known the mind of the Lord? Or who has been his counselor?" (Romans 11:33-34).

One should also know what Martin Luther said about reason at the end of his life. Man's reason (his thinking abilities) can often lead a person astray. Man's reason is like a harlot which can deceive us, unless the Word of God leads us.[9] Where Scripture speaks, we should listen in faith. We should teach and believe what Scripture teaches, even though our reason cannot fully understand it.

One should also be thankful that if he loves the Lord, then he is already elect. God has already worked in his heart.

We should thank God for choosing and loving us. Then we should go out and preach the Gospel so that others may hear and believe too. For maybe they are elect too! God's Spirit uses people like you and me to bring others into his Kingdom. A belief in God's election does not exclude human responsibility.

Study Questions

1. What is the ordinary meaning and the theological meaning of election? How many elections can you think of in the Bible?
2. What is the relationship between divine sovereignty and human responsibility? How do these two doctrines relate to you as a Christian?
3. What is irresistible grace? What is the relationship between irresistible grace and election?
4. What is total depravity? Who is totally depraved?
5. How can the perseverance of the saints be a comfort to you?
6. What are the arguments for limited atonement?
7. List the Five Points of Calvinism, using the acronym TULIP.

---

[9] "The Last Sermon in Wittenberg 1546," *Luther's Works* 51:371-80.

Chapter Twelve

God's Lordship in History: Providence

In the last chapter we saw that God is active in our salvation. In this chapter, we will see how God is active in our daily lives. This is the doctrine of providence.

The doctrine of providence says that when God created the world, he did not abandon it, but he continues to sustain and govern it. Calvin says that we believe that God is not just the Creator of all but "he is also the everlasting Governor and Preserver" of the world. God "sustains, nourishes and cares for everything he has made, even to the least sparrow."[10]

Providence is the belief in the rule of God in the world; it is the belief that God cares for and directs the course of history.

There are two parts to God's providence. First, God cares for and sustains the world of nature. Psalm 104 is a beautiful psalm which says that God provides water for the fields and the animals; all the animals look to God and he "gives them food at their proper time" (vs. 27). In Matthew 10:29-30, Jesus says that our Father cares for the little birds of the field and he even watches over the hairs on our head. Again, Paul, when he was in Lystra, said that God "has shown kindness by giving you rain from heaven and crops in their

---

[10] *Institutes* I.16.1; pp. 197-98. Calvin deals with providence in a full way in *Institutes* I.16-18 (Book I, chs. 16-18), pp. 197-237. This section is worthwhile reading.

seasons; he provides you with plenty of food and fills your hearts with joy" (Acts 14:17). This is one part of providence, whereby God keeps the world running smoothly.

The second part of providence is God's acting in human history. The Bible teaches that God controls and directs the events of history. He is Lord in history and he acts for the benefit of his people.

God's involvement in history is an example of divine sovereignty. God is Lord in history, causing events to happen.

At the same time, every person is responsible for what he does. We are responsible for our actions. This is called human responsibility. We cannot blame God for the evil we do, for we are responsible for our actions.

The Reformed faith holds to both divine sovereignty and human responsibility. Both God and man are acting in the very same events of history.

The Bible gives many examples of God acting in history. After Joseph's brothers sold him into Egyptian captivity, Joseph said that it was really God who sent him to Egypt. God did this for the purpose of saving lives (Gen. 45:5-8). He also said: "You intended to harm me, but God intended it for good to accomplish what is now being done, the saving of many lives" (Gen. 50:20).

This is a classic example of divine sovereignty and human responsibility working at the same time. Joseph's brothers did something evil to their brother by selling him into captivity; they were responsible for their wicked deeds. But God was in control and he used this evil deed to accomplish good, namely, the feeding of many people during the seven years of famine. This activity of God is an example of divine sovereignty. Both man and God were involved in the selling of Joseph into captivity, but their intentions were different.

Another example of providence is found in Isaiah 10:5-11. There Assyria is called the rod of God's anger (vs. 5).

God sent Assyria against Israel to punish her for her wicked ways. This activity of God is an example of God's sovereignty. God's purpose was good, to discipline his people, even though Assyria's purpose was evil. The armies of Assyria wanted to seize land and gold and treasures; they killed and looted. This is an example of man's freedom or responsibility. The Assyrians were responsible for their evil acts. But since God is Lord of history, he was able to use an evil army like that of Assyria to accomplish his good goal of disciplining Israel.

A further example of providence is the killing of Jesus. Who put Jesus to death? Peter says that "Herod and Pontius Pilate met together with the Gentiles and the people of Israel" to plot against Jesus (Acts 4:27). Herod, Pilate, some Gentiles and some Jews killed Jesus. Since the crucifixion was done by human beings, we call it part of human responsibility. But it was also something that God caused to happen. The next verse says that "they did what [God's] power and will had decided beforehand should happen" (vs. 28). This is divine sovereignty. So God and man put Jesus to death, but for different reasons: God did it so that we might have salvation; but the people did it because they did not like Jesus. (Acts 2:23 explains the same thing. Peter says that wicked people put Jesus to death, but this happened in "God's set purpose and foreknowledge.")

Many other examples from the Bible can be mentioned to show how God works in history. All of these examples illustrate providence, which is God's acting and governing in history and in our daily lives.

The word providence comes from the word "provide." This shows us what God's purpose is in ruling in history. The main purpose of providence is to protect and provide for God's people, the church. The doctrine of providence gives comfort to the believer. If God cares for the small birds and even counts the hairs of our head, then: "Don't be afraid; you are worth more than many sparrows" (Matt. 10:31). If God cares for the birds of the air and the flowers of the field, will he not care for us? Therefore we should not worry (Matt. 6:25-34).

Essentially providence is the statement of faith that "in all things God works for the good of those who love him, who have been called according to his purpose" (Rom. 8:28). Therefore we do not have to fear death or life, angels or principalities, or anything else (vss. 38-39).

Of course, this doctrine is not without difficulties. If there is providence or God's rule in history, why is there evil? We don't really know the answer to this. We don't know precisely how God works in history. But we do know that throughout history there is often a simultaneous activity of both God and man.

We should not try to answer all the questions concerning providence because no one knows exactly how and why God acts in history and in our lives. But as Christians we do believe that God works on our behalf and therefore all things work together for our good if we believe in him and trust in him.

Study Questions

1. Define providence. What are the two parts of providence?
2. How did God and man both act in the taking of Israel into Assyrian captivity?
3. Explain how human responsibility and divine sovereignty can both be seen in the crucifixion of Jesus.
4. How is the doctrine of providence a comfort to the believer?
5. If we sin, is it our fault or God's fault? Explain.

Chapter Thirteen

God's Lordship in the Christian Life: Sanctification

The lordship of God is the most important idea in Calvinism. We have seen above that God is Lord in the conversion process; he is also Lord in history. In this chapter we will look at his lordship in our daily lives. Since Christ is King, our lives have to be lived in obedience to him. This chapter will look at sanctification or the Christian life.

Christian theology believes that there are two parts to the Christian life: justification and sanctification. Justification is the legal righteousness that we receive through faith because of the saving work of Jesus. Sanctification is the Christian life of good works that we live once we have believed and have been justified.

We can talk of two parts to sanctification. There is the sanctification of the individual Christian; there is also the sanctification or transformation of society. We will look at both of these.

Individual Sanctification

When the Reformation began, Martin Luther strongly emphasized justification by faith alone. He stressed this because the Roman Catholic Church was saying that salvation comes through faith and works, not just faith. The Catholic church was selling indulgences which would help a person get salvation. People were paying money to get salvation. The Catholics were teaching that one can be saved through faith and works.

Luther responded by saying that you cannot buy your way into heaven. He said that good works will not save a person. Instead, we are saved only by grace through faith (Eph. 2:8).

All Protestants, including Calvin, agreed with Luther on this point. But Calvin was born 26 years after Luther, and he began his ministry about 25 years later than Luther. Luther was a first-generation Reformer; Calvin was a second-generation Reformer.

At the time of Calvin, some of the Catholics were accusing the Lutherans of not caring about good works. They said that because Lutherans believed in justification by faith and not by works, they did not care about works. This accusation was usually wrong. Protestants believe that works are important in the Christian life.

So while Calvin agreed with Luther on justification by faith, he stressed sanctification. While justification by faith is at the heart of Luther's theology, sanctification is central to Calvin.

We can see this in Calvin's *Institutes*. Normally a theologian first talks of justification and then sanctification. However Calvin reverses this order. In Book 3 of the *Institutes* Calvin first talks of sanctification (in Chapters 3-10) and then only secondly of justification (in Chapters 11-18).

Calvin obviously thought that the pressing need for the Reformed church was sanctification. Everyone accepted justification; but there were problems in the church on the issue of the Christian life.

People were asking questions like: "Why is it important to live a holy and Christian life? If we are justified by faith, may we not go out and sin as we like?" Calvin's answer is related to the kingship of Christ. If Christ is King, then we should not live sinful lives. If Christ is King, then sanctification and good works are essential.

In Book 3, Chapter 7 of the *Institutes*, Calvin says that we are not our own, but we are God's. If we are not our own, we should flee from sin. If we are God's, "let us therefore live for him and die for him." "We are God's: let all the parts of our life accordingly strive toward him as our only lawful goal." He says that Christianity teaches one to "submit and subject [himself] to the Holy Spirit so that the man himself may ... hear Christ living and reigning within him."[11]

This is a beautiful passage that you should find and read. We are reminded that we should live a Christian life because we belong to God and because Christ reigns in us.

Calvin put these ideas into practice in Geneva. Since Christ is Lord, sin had no place in the city where Calvin lived and worked. The consistory of the Reformed church in Geneva closely watched the lives of the church members. If major sins were committed, the consistory put the members under discipline. If the sins continued, excommunication followed.

John Knox put the same principles into practice in the Presbyterian church in Scotland. The table of the Lord was open only to those who were not practicing any major and obvious sins.

Of course the Scottish and Genevan churches sometimes carried discipline too far. But there was a genuine belief that since Christ is King, the Christian community needs to live a sincere and holy life.

---

[11] *Institutes* III.7.1; p. 690.

The Lordship of God in Society

The kingship of Christ has implications for society as well. Since Christ is King, all of life must be subject to his rule. Social life as well as individual life must be made holy.

Many Christians only talk of individual sanctification. These Christians often say that it is wrong to get involved in politics. Many of these Christians are pietistic. Pietism believes that Christianity is only personal piety. Reformed Christians believes that piety is very important, but Christianity is more than personal piety.

The Reformed position says that since Christ is Lord over everything, Christians should try to transform society. Both the individual and the society must be sanctified.

Abraham Kuyper was a Dutch theologian who taught the lordship of Christ over all of life.[12] Kuyper said that in human life there are many areas or spheres. There are the spheres of the family, the church institute, the school, the work place, the government, recreation and art, just to name a few. Each sphere has its own task. The government rules the people; the family raises children; the church preaches and evangelizes; the work force produces products like food and clothing; the sports organizations allow people to relax and exercise their bodies.

Abraham Kuyper says that each area of life should be separate from the other, but they should also be interrelated. He calls this "sphere sovereignty."[13] The church institute

---

[12] The end of chapter 5 discusses Abraham Kuyper.

[13] In 1880 when the Free University of Amsterdam was inaugurated, Abraham Kuyper delivered a speech called *Souvereiniteit in eigen kring* (Sovereignty in Each Sphere).

should not be governing the nation; the factory should not be educating children; the schools should not be manufacturing goods. But to have a good society, all of these spheres must cooperate.

Although every sphere is sovereign in its own area, Kuyper firmly believed that Jesus Christ is sovereign over each sphere. Every area of life should be Christian. We have already seen Kuyper's powerful statement that "there is not a single square inch of the entire universe of which Christ the sovereign Lord of all does not say,'This is mine!'" Christ is thus Lord over all of life.

Sometimes this lordship of Christ is not recognized. Then God is ruling only in a general sense. But where Christ's lordship is recognized in any sphere of life, then we can talk of the presence of God's Kingdom in that area.

If a school teaches its children according to Biblical principles, then God's Kingdom is present. If a government practices justice and mercy, then there are glimpses of Christ's Kingdom. If a family raises its children in the fear of the Lord, there Christ's Kingdom is visible. If a church organization faithfully does its work, the Kingdom of God is present.

Obviously, God's Kingdom will be present in this world in an imperfect way. The Kingdom of God will reach perfection only in the age to come. But we should recognize that God's Kingdom is present in all of life, and not just in our church organizations. God's Kingdom is also present outside the visible church.

Many of the principles of this vision were laid down by John Calvin himself. Calvin believed in the glory and majesty of God, and he tried to realize God's glory in his own society. We have seen that Calvin tried to make Geneva a Christian city. He was concerned that all the citizens of the city of Geneva would live Christian lives. He wanted Jesus to reign in Geneva.

Calvin was also concerned that other cities and countries in Europe would become Christian. In his preface to the *Institutes*, which was addressed to King Francis I of France, Calvin said that a true king is one who "recognizes himself a minister of God in governing his kingdom. Now, that king who in ruling over his realm does not serve God's glory does not exercise kingly rule but brigandage [robbery]."[14] In other words, the king must serve God in his government. (How many Christian politicians today serve God in their politics?)

Calvin wrote similar things to other kings of Europe. In 1552, he wrote to Edward VI, King of England, commending him for being a Christian king and calling him a "lieutenant in ordering and maintaining the kingdom of Jesus Christ in England." Calvin told Edward that he should be an example to his subjects by submitting to Jesus Christ, that great King, and that he should submit to the spiritual scepter of the Gospel.[15]

In 1555 Calvin wrote the King of Poland reminding him of the command in Psalm 2 where "kings are commanded to embrace the Son of God," which means that they are to obey Christ.[16]

In addition to these letters to the kings of France, England and Poland, Calvin wrote other political leaders in Europe in his time. Calvin was insistent that Christ is Lord over earthly kings and that political rulers must always obey Christ.

---

[14] *Institutes*, p. 12.

[15] *Letters of John Calvin*, I:355.

[16] *Letters of John Calvin*, II:245.

The Reformed faith has a world-and-life view. All of the world and all of life belongs under the rule of God. All of life is religious. The Kingdom of God extends across all spheres of life. But so does the Kingdom of Satan. There is thus spiritual warfare between the two kingdoms. The task of the Christian is to redeem all parts of life for Jesus and to bring all parts of life under Christ's lordship.

The Law of God

If the Christian life is so important, how do we know how to live this life? Obviously the Holy Spirit guides us in the Christian life. John 16:13 calls the Holy Spirit the "Spirit of truth" who "will guide you into all truth." Calvin believed this to be true.

Calvin also always said that Word and Spirit must work together. If you have the Word without the Spirit, you have dead legalism. But if you have the Spirit without the Word, then you run the danger of emotionalism and subjectivity.

Maybe someone claims that the Spirit tells him in a special revelation to divorce his wife. Calvin would answer: What does the Word of God say? The Word of God says that divorce is wrong. Further, the Holy Spirit cannot contradict the Word of God that he has written. Therefore, the person's revelation is a false revelation. Always listen to the Word of God and the Holy Spirit at the same time! Word and Spirit belong together in the Christian life!

The Word of God is essential in knowing how to live the Christian life. In particular, the law of God guides a person. The Reformed faith has always had a high regard for God's law.

One can distinguish three types of laws in the Bible. The ceremonial law deals with sacrifices and priestly rituals. Most of these laws no longer apply to us because Christ is the final sacrifice. There are also political laws that applied to the nation of Israel and do not apply to us today. But the moral laws in the Bible still apply to us today in principle. For example, we should not kill, steal or commit adultery; we should care for the poor and the orphan; and, in summary, we should love God and love our neighbor. The principles of these moral laws apply to every person in every age.

Calvin taught that the moral law has three functions or purposes.[17] First, the law warns people that they are sinful and that therefore they need salvation in Jesus. Second, the law restrains evil persons to some extent. "The third and principal use" of the law "finds its place among believers in whose hearts the Spirit of God already lives and reigns."[18] The law helps guide Christians in their Christian life.

This emphasis on the law is a characteristic part of Reformed and Presbyterian liturgies. Often in the church service, we read either the Law (often the Ten Commandments) or a summary of the Law from Matthew 22:34-40. If the reading of the Law comes before a confession of sin, then the Law is being used to point us to Christ for the forgiveness of sins. This is the first use of the Law. But if the Law comes after a confession of sins, then the Law reminds us of how to live the Christian life. This is the third use of the law.

The Reformed faith has always said that God's law is good. Paul states this clearly in Romans 7:12-14. In Galatians, Paul says that the law is bad if it is used as a way of

---

[17] *Institutes* II.7.6-13; pp. 354-362.

[18] *Institutes* II.7.12; p. 360.

salvation; but it is good as a guide for the Christian life. The law helps us to live a life of holiness or sanctification. The law helps us to know what Christ our King wants us to do.

Study questions

1. Why did Calvin emphasize sanctification more than Luther?
2. Why should we live a Christian life?
3. What did Abraham Kuyper mean with "sphere sovereignty"?
4. How did Calvin apply the idea of the kingship of Christ to the city of Geneva?
5. How should Nigerian rulers apply the doctrine of the lordship of Christ in this country?
6. Why is it dangerous to listen to the Holy Spirit without reading the Word of God?
7. How is the third use of the law helpful in your life?

Chapter Fourteen

God's Lordship in the Church

The rule of Christ can be seen in many areas of life. But it is in the visible church that Christ's rule shines most clearly. In the visible church people willingly acknowledge and confess the name of Jesus. In the church the Word of God is regularly preached.

The fourth Book or part of Calvin's *Institutes* deals with the church. Calvin was writing at the time when the Roman Catholic Church was particularly corrupt. So Calvin, like Wyclif, Hus and Luther, distinguished between the visible and invisible church.[19] The invisible church is all the people who are true believers. The visible church is the institution or organization which includes both the true believers and the hypocrites (or nominal believers). Our own churches (PCN, CRCN, ERCC, NKST, NRC, RCCN, QIC) are visible parts of the church.

It is probably better to talk of the visible and invisible dimensions or sides of the one church of Christ. Christ's church is one, with a visible and an invisible side.

Only God knows who the true members of the church are; these true members make up the invisible side of the church. They are the elect, known certainly only by God.

---

[19] *Institutes* IV.1.7, p. 1021-22. These pages are important reading.

The church in its invisible side becomes visible to the world through its activities. The true believers will form church organizations; they will have presidents or general secretaries; they will have pastors and church buildings; they will take names and register themselves with the government. These visible activities are the part of the visible side of the church.

We can visualize the two dimensions of the church as two concentric circles. The bigger circle is the visible church. It has both believers and hypocrites (nominal believers) in it. The smaller circle inside the bigger circle would be the invisible church or the true believers or the elect.

During his time, Calvin wanted to distinguish between true churches and false churches. Calvin said that a true church was one that was faithful to Jesus; a false church was not.

Calvin said that one should look for marks or signs to see whether a church is a true church. He spoke of two marks of the church: the pure preaching of the Word and the correct administration of the sacraments.[20] (The First Scots Confession and the Belgic Confession made discipline a third mark of the church.)

In the Catholic church of Calvin's day, the Word was not being truly preached and the sacraments were not being properly administered. Therefore Calvin concluded that the Catholic church was not a true church, even though there were still traces of the true church in the Catholic church.[21] (Today the Catholic church is not as obviously a false church as it was in the time of Calvin.)

---

[20] *Institutes*, IV.1.9, p. 1023.

[21] *Institutes*, IV.2; pp. 1041 ff.

Church Government

Scripture teaches that Christ is the head of the church (e.g., Eph. 5:23). Calvin was in full agreement with this. He said that Christ "alone should rule and reign in the church..., and this authority should be exercised and administered by his Word alone."[22] Calvin called the Word of God the scepter of Christ the King. Christ ruled by his Word as it is preached from Sunday to Sunday. Calvin had a high regard for the preaching of the Word. He believed that the Word of God, through the Holy Spirit, can transform lives.

We believe that all power in the church belongs to Jesus Christ. But since he is not visibly present, he entrusts power to the church and its officers. We believe in the priesthood of all believers. The congregation as a whole has received power from Christ, yet the congregation elects officers to lead and govern it.

We believe that today there are three basic offices in the church: the office of pastor, elder and deacon. Each officer has his special duty.

The **pastor** is the spiritual leader of the church. His task is to preach the Word of God faithfully every Sunday. He is to encourage the believers in their faith. He is to give leadership and direction to the church.

Calvin said that the pastor should be held in high respect for it is he who brings the Word of God to the people. And, as we have seen, Christ rules through his Word.

The apostle Paul also teaches that apostles and pastors have rights. Paul writes: "Don't we have the right to food and drink? ... Who serves as a soldier at his own expense? Who

---

[22] *Institutes*, IV.3.1; p. 1053.

plants a vineyard and does not eat of its grapes? Who tends a flock and does not drink of the milk? ... If we have sown spiritual seed among you, is it too much if we reap a material harvest from you?" (1 Cor. 9:3-11). Scripture teaches that the worker deserves a fair wage.

On the other hand, the worker must work faithfully. In the same passage, Paul says: "Woe to me if I do not preach the gospel! ... Though I am free and belong to no man, I make myself a slave to everyone, to win as many as possible. ... I have become all things to all men so that by all possible means I might save some" (1 Cor. 9:16-22).

The relationship between the pastor and the church is like a marriage relationship. If the husband treats the wife in love, the wife will cook good soup. Then the husband might give his wife money for new clothes. But if the husband treats the wife poorly, the wife might cook poor soup. Then the husband might spend his money outside of the house.

So it is with the church. If the pastor serves faithfully, the church will often thank him with a good salary and maybe by working on his farm. But if the pastor lords it over the church and treats the members unkindly, then the church will not respond in kindness to him.

This leads us to the second office in the church, that of **elder.** The New Testament has two Greek words for elder. One word is *presbuteros*, which means older man or elder. (The name Presbyterian comes from this word.) The other word is *episkopos*, which sounds like the word bishop. The word episcopal comes from this word. But the original meaning of *episkopos* was not bishop, but overseer. *Skopos* means to look; *epi* means over. In other words, the overseer is to govern or oversee the work of the church. In the New Testament time, there were no bishops, so bishop is a wrong translation for *episkopos*. The early church began to have bishops only in the second century.

It is clear in the New Testament that "elder" and "overseer" are two words to describe those who rule the church. This is clear from Paul's farewell talk to the Ephesian elders. In Acts 20:17, Paul calls the elders (*presbuteroi*) of the church of Ephesus to meet him at Miletus. Paul tells them that he will be leaving them and that they will have to take care of the church. He says: "Guard yourselves and all the flock of which the Holy Spirit has made you overseers (*episkopoi*). Be shepherds of the church of God" (vs. 28).

Two things are clear from this passage. First, the words elder and overseer refer to the same group of people. Secondly, the task of the elder or overseer is to take care of the church. Of course, the elder does this together with the pastor. The elders and pastor must work together in building up the church of Christ.

1 Timothy 3:1-7 and Titus 1:6-9 give the qualifications for an elder. (1 Timothy calls him an overseer; Titus calls him an elder; but of course the two are the same.) An elder must be a man of good standing in the church. He must be "above reproach, the husband of but one wife, temperate, self-controlled, respectable, hospitable, able to teach, not given to much wine, not violent but gentle, not quarrelsome, not a lover of money" (1 Tim. 3:2-3). These are strong words! Paul is here saying that the leaders of the church should be of outstanding character.

Too often in our churches, both pastors and elders think that an office is a source of power for themselves. They like to lord it over others, either the church members or other officers. Sometimes the elders treat the pastor as unimportant; sometimes the pastor treats the elders as ignorant people.

The Bible says that both pastor and elder should be treated with respect. The Bible also teaches "servant leadership." The leader is to be a servant to the church and to Christ. Jesus gave us an example of this in John 13 when he washed the disciples feet. He said: "Now that I, your Lord and Teacher, have washed your feet, you also should wash one another's feet" (John 13:14). Jesus also criticized his disciples who wanted the best places in the Kingdom of God. He said that in the world "those who are regarded as rulers of the Gentiles lord it over them." But "not so with you...Whoever wants to become great among you must be your servant" (Mark 10:42-43).

Too often our church leaders act like the rulers of the Gentiles that Jesus is describing. We need to remember two things: the office of pastor and elder is a high calling; but pastors and elders have been called to serve the church and her Lord and Master.

The third office in our Reformed and Presbyterian system is that of **deacon**. The Greek word for deacon is *diakonos*, which means helper or servant. It is commonly assumed that the origin of the office of deacon is found in Acts 6 although the word deacon is not found there. In this chapter, the Greek Jews complained that their widows were not being properly taken care of. The twelve apostles said that they were too busy with the ministry of the Word to wait on tables. So they chose seven men, including Stephen, to take care of the poor and needy in the church.

In our Reformed and Presbyterian system, the deacons manage the church money and they take care of the needy in the church. 1 Timothy 3:8-13 gives the qualifications for the office of deacon. They are similar to the elder's qualifications. Deacons too should be people of good moral character.

In the Presbyterian and Reformed system, local congregations in a certain area are organized into a presbytery or a classis. The presbyteries or classes are sometimes united into a regional church council. These bodies are then united into a general assembly or a synod. These broader assemblies help the church make a united witness in our society. They also help regulate the life of the church both in doctrine and in practice. We believe that strength is found in unity. Therefore if Christians of a same faith unite, the church will be stronger.

The Sacraments of Baptism and the Lord's Supper

The Reformed and Presbyterian churches believe that there are only two sacraments instituted by Christ. Our churches reject five of the seven sacraments of the Roman Catholic Church. We believe that baptism and the Lord's Supper are the two sacraments that Christ instituted.

A sacrament is a holy ordinance instituted by Christ in which the grace of God in Christ is signified (or pictured by a sign) and sealed for believers.[23] There are two important elements to a sacrament: it is both a sign and a seal.

First of all, a sacrament is a sign. A sign is something visible that is a picture of something else. A sign which says "Makurdi" is not Makurdi itself but it shows us where Makurdi is. A picture of a bird is not the bird itself, but a sign of the bird. In the same way the sacraments are signs.

Baptism is a sign that our sins are washed away. When water is poured on a person or when the person enters water, it is a picture of the washing away of our sins. The Lord's Supper is also a sign or a picture. The broken bread and poured wine are pictures of the broken body and the shed

---

[23] This is a simple version of the definition by Louis Berkhof in his *Systematic Theology*, p. 617.

blood of Jesus that were given for our sins. When we eat the bread and drink the cup, we have a picture of Jesus who is our spiritual food.

But the sacraments are also seals. At the Theological College of Northern Nigeria, we have a college seal. We use the seal on official documents like graduation certificates. The seal indicates that this certificate is an official one that has our blessing.

In the same way, baptism and the Lord's Supper are seals. In baptism, God seals that the baptized person belongs to him. In the Lord's Supper, God seals the believing person to himself when the person eats and drinks in faith.

Of course, the sacraments are not magic. They are not an absolute guarantee of salvation. If one is baptized, it does not mean that he is saved. If one eats and drinks at the Lord's Supper, he is not automatically part of God's Kingdom.

However, we believe that through the sacraments the person is strengthened in his faith. We believe that the Holy Spirit is present and that he will bless the person if the person (or the infant's parents) has faith.

If faith is so important, then why do we baptize infants? Obviously they do not have an active faith when they are babies. To answer this question, we have to know what baptism is.

Baptism is an initiation rite into the family of God. When a person believes in Christ, he is baptized as a sign that he is now part of the people of God or the church. Baptism in the New Testament is like circumcision in the Old Testament.

In Genesis 17 we have the story of how God made a covenant or an agreement with Abraham. The covenant is a relationship between God and Abraham. It is summed up in the words of God: "I will be your God, and you will be my people." (You can see this formula in Jeremiah 31:33.) A covenant is like a marriage relationship where two persons promise to love each other and be faithful to each other.

In Genesis 17, God promised to bless Abraham and to be his God (vss. 3-8). Then, in verses 9-14, God expected Abraham to keep the covenant. In other words, Abraham had to obey God in everything. Abraham also had to be circumcised because circumcision is "the sign of the covenant" (vs. 11). In other words, circumcision is a sign that the person belongs to God. Circumcision is the initiation rite into fellowship with God.

It was important that all the male children were circumcised. This meant that children were included among the people of God. They were part of the covenant. They were part of the family of God. In the Old Testament children were part of God's people.

(It is clear that both boys and girls were part of the covenant in the Old Testament even though the girls were not circumcised. The Bible does not approve of female circumcision. Female circumcision is an offense against the person of a woman, and it should be strongly discouraged.)

In the Old Testament children were part of the family of God. Surely, then, in the New Testament children of believers are also part of God's family. Surely, they are members of the church. If they are members, obviously they need to be baptized as a sign of their membership.

Children who are baptized are called baptized members. When they make a public profession of faith, then we call them professing members. Our churches believe that a person who is baptized as a child should make a public profession of his faith in Jesus so that we may know that he or she is a true member of the church.

Once a person makes a public profession of faith, then he is welcome to partake of the Lord's Supper. We believe that the Lord's Supper is more than just a symbol or a sign that Jesus died for us. We believe that our faith is strengthened in the Lord's Supper by the Holy Spirit. The Lord's Supper seals us in the family of God.

We believe that Jesus is present at the Lord's Supper. However he is present in his divine nature, not in his body. We believe that the body of Jesus is in heaven since the physical body of Jesus is not omnipresent. The divine nature of Christ is obviously present everywhere. As Calvin said, we cannot imagine that the Word or the eternal Son could be confined in an earthly body.[24] We believe that Christ is present through his divine nature when we partake of the Supper, and it is this nature that strengthens us in our faith.

During the Reformation period, there was a discussion about the presence of Christ in the Lord's Supper. The Roman Catholics taught transubstantiation. This means that the bread and wine become the body and blood of Jesus every time the Lord's Supper is held. The Roman Catholics thus believed that Jesus is sacrificed again every time the Lord's Supper is celebrated. However we believe that Christ was sacrificed only once, at Calvary, and not every time there is communion.

The Lutherans believe in consubstantiation. They believe that Christ's body and divine nature are present at the Lord's Supper. However we believe that Christ's body is not omnipresent.

Zwingli believed that the Lord's Supper was just a sign or symbol of the death of Christ and not a seal. We believe that the Supper is both a sign and a seal.

It is useful to know about the differences among the Protestants about the Lord's Supper. But we do not think that

---

[24] *Institutes* II.13.4 (p. 481); cf. *Institutes* IV.17.30 (pp. 1401-1403).

relatively small differences of doctrine should divide the Christian body. The Lord's Supper is called communion; it should be a symbol of Christian unity. We should be aware of what we believe, but we should not let the communion divide us!

Study Questions

1. What is the visible side of your church? What is the invisible side of your church?
2. Who is the head of your church?
3. Why do problems arise so often between pastors and elders in our churches?
4. What is the difference between overseer and elder?
5. Why should we baptize children of believers?
6. How is the Lord's Supper a sign? How is it a seal?
7. Is Christ present when we celebrate the Lord's Supper? How is he present?

Chapter Fifteen

God's Lordship in the Future: Eschatology

The kingship of Christ is central to Reformed and Presbyterian theology. We believe that when Jesus came upon this earth, he established his Kingdom, although it began in a small way like a mustard seed. At the same time we believe that the kingdom of Satan is also strong. There is spiritual warfare between the two kingdoms.

We believe that the reign of Christ is universal, and yet not everyone recognizes this authority. In the world there are two groups of people: those who obey Christ and those who do not. Everyone belongs either to the Kingdom of God or the kingdom of Satan.

Scripture also teaches that at the end "every knee shall bow ... and every tongue confess that Jesus Christ is Lord" (Phil. 2:10-11). At the end the devil and his followers shall be thrown into the pit of fire (Rev. 20:10). Then "the kingdom of the world [will] become the kingdom of our Lord and of his Christ, and he will reign for ever and ever" (Rev. 11:15).

Eschatology is the study of the last things. Reformed eschatology believes that in the future Christ's reign and his Kingdom will be brought to completion. These beliefs are also held by all Christians.

However, Christians disagree about some of the events preceding the end. What will happen before Jesus comes again? What will happen when he comes again? These are difficult questions.

Jesus himself said that there would be signs before he returned In Matthew 24, Jesus said there would be wars, rumors of wars, famines, earthquakes, persecution, false prophets, tribulation and great distress. We know that many of these signs are with us now. But many of these things have been happening since the time of Jesus. In A.D. 70, when Jerusalem was destroyed, some of these prophecies were partially fulfilled.

Matthew 24 also reminds us that Jesus would come as a thief in the night. Jesus will come when we do not expect him (vs. 44). We should not develop too detailed theories about when Jesus will come again.

The Book of Revelation is another book that talks about the future. Revelation is of course a difficult book to understand. We should remember, though, that Revelation is apocalyptic literature, using a great deal of symbolism. Numbers are usually symbolic; many of the events described will not happen in exactly the way they are described. We must read Revelation carefully and prayerfully to understand the deeper meaning of many of these passages.[25]

We should also know that the author uses parallelism in Revelation. The seven seals, trumpets and bowls do not describe three different set of events. Instead, they describe part of world history from three points of view.

---

[25] Two classic Reformed commentaries on Revelation are: Wm. Hendriksen, *More than Conquerors* (Grand Rapids, 1940); and Harry Boer, *A Guide to the Book of Revelation* (Achimota, 1978).

The Millennium

The most controversial part of Revelation is probably chapter 20. This is the chapter that talks about the thousand-year reign, or the millennium. (Millennium means thousand years in the Latin language.)

Revelation 20 gives a picture of an angel coming down from heaven. The angel seizes Satan and throws him into a pit for a thousand years. After the thousand years, Satan will be set free for a short time.

During the thousand years, the souls of those who were beheaded will reign with Christ. After the thousand years, Satan will be released from prison. There will then be a great battle, in which fire will come from heaven and destroy Satan and his hosts. They will be thrown into the lake of fire. After that will be the last judgment. (You should read Revelation 20 carefully to see exactly what it says.)

The main question about this chapter is: When are the thousand years? Will Christ return before or after the thousand years?

There are three main answers to these questions. There are the post-millennial, pre-millennial and a-millennial points of view. We will look at them in this order.[26]

Post-millennialists say that Christ will come *after* ("post") a literal thousand years of spiritual peace and prosperity. Many believe that the thousand years began in the nineteenth century, at the time of the great worldwide missionary movement. They think that we are now enjoying such a worldwide spiritual prosperity. But most people today

---

[26] The best Reformed source on this issue is: Anthony Hoekema, *The Bible and the Future* (Grand Rapids, 1979).

say that there is too much evil in the world for this theory to be true.

Pre-millennialists say that Christ will come *before* ("pre") the thousand years. Pre-millennial dispensationalists believe that Christ will come and take only the believers up to heaven in the rapture. They believe that there will then be seven years of tribulation. During this time many Jews will believe. At the end of the seven years Christ will come again to set up a thousand year kingdom on earth. At the end of the thousand years there will be the final judgment.

This pre-millennial position is held by many believers today. But these people make some basic mistakes. The Bible says that there will only be one future coming of Jesus, not two comings. The Bible says that when Jesus comes again, the dead will be raised and Christ will judge the world. It is wrong to say that Jesus will come two times in the future. It is wrong to say that there will be a thousand years between his future coming and the last judgment. The Bible teaches that there are just two ages: the present age and the age to come.

The pre-millennial position makes the mistake of reading the Book of Revelation in a literal way. Revelation is special prophetic literature called apocalyptic literature. There is much symbolism in Revelation. The numbers of Revelation are often symbolic. Obviously the number one thousand is symbolic, referring to a long period of time. It is wrong to say that one thousand years is literal.

The Reformed and Presbyterian position is called a-millennial. (The Latin prefix "a" means "no." We believe that there will be *no* literal thousand year reign.) Probably a better term for our thinking is "realized millennium," because we believe that the millennium is now. Christ is reigning now!

He is at the right hand of the Father, and he has all authority (Eph. 1:20-23; Mt. 28:18-20). We believe that he began his reign at the ascension and he will finish his reign at the Last Judgment, when he hands back the authority to the Father (1 Cor. 15:24-28). Christ is now reigning through his Word and his Spirit.

Wherever Christ's name is acknowledged, he is reigning. If we look at the world, we will see that there are churches in almost every country of the world. Christ's reign is global! In Nigeria, at least half the population is Christian. Evil spirits are being cast out, people understand principles of justice, and the poor are being cared for.

We believe that we are in the millennium now! We believe that the millennium began with the ascension of Christ and it will finish when Christ comes again at the Last Day. The Kingdom of God is here, as the Gospels tell us. When Jesus came, he said: "Repent, for the Kingdom of Heaven is at hand" (Mt. 4:17). Jesus said that when demons are cast out, the Kingdom of God is here (Mt. 12:28). He said that the Kingdom of God is like a mustard seed which is already growing (Mt. 13:31-32). So the Kingdom is present because Christ is reigning.

The millennium is the reign of Christ between his first and second comings when he is reigning. The millennium is now!

Of course there is evil in the world, but Christ's name is also being glorified. When Revelation 20:2 says that Satan was thrown into the pit at the beginning of the thousand years, this means that the power of Satan was limited after Jesus ascended into heaven. As Jesus said in Luke 10:18 when demons were cast out: "I saw Satan fall like lightning from heaven."

We should remember that before Jesus came, Satan's kingdom was strongly established throughout the world, except in the tiny country of Israel. But when Jesus came, the Gospel rapidly spread throughout the Roman Empire and beyond. The binding of Satan began with the first coming of Christ.

We believe that Scripture talks about tribulation and persecution. We do not think that there will be a single seven-year period of tribulation in the future. (The number seven in Revelation is usually symbolic.) John, who wrote Revelation, experienced persecution. We see tribulation today in Nigeria. Many Reformed people also believe that there will be intense persecution before Christ comes again. Then the powers of the antichrist will be seen.

Then, sometime in the future, Christ will come again. Satan and his hosts will be defeated instantly. This is what the Bible means by the battle of Armageddon (Rev. 16:16) or the battle of Gog and Magog (Ezek. 38-39; Rev. 20:7-9). This will not be a long battle: Satan will be defeated at once.

The coming of Christ will be with a loud command and a trumpet call (1 Thess. 4:16). It will be a loud and noisy event. There will be no secret rapture. First the dead will rise; then the believers who are alive will be caught up with Christ in the clouds (1 Thess. 4:16-17).

When Christ comes in this noisy way, he will gather his own to himself. "Two men will be in the field; one will be taken and the other left. Two women will be grinding with a hand mill; one will be taken and the other left" (Mt. 24:39-40). This will happen at his final coming.

We Reformed Christians look forward to one final event when Christ will appear, when Satan will be defeated, and when the believers will be taken to be with Christ.

Then Christ's Kingdom will be fully established. Then we will enter the new Jerusalem, described in Revelation 21 and 22. "There will be no more death or mourning or crying or pain, for the old order of things has passed away" (Rev.

21:4). In the center of this city will be the throne of God and of the Lamb. The saints will reign with God for ever and ever (Rev. 22:3-5).

This is the future Kingdom of God for which we wait. "He who testifies to these things says,'Yes, I am coming soon.' Amen. Come Lord Jesus" (Rev. 22:20).

Study questions

1. According to Matthew 24, when will there be tribulation?
2. When is the thousand-year reign according to the Reformed position? Where does Christ reign, according to this position?
3. How many future returns of Christ does the pre-millennial position teach? How many future comings does the Reformed position teach? What does the Bible say?
4. Does the Bible teach a secret and silent rapture? When will the believers be taken to be with Christ?
5. According to Revelation 20:7-10, when will Satan be released? When will the battle of Gog and Magog be? How will it be fought?
6. What does a-millennial mean? Why is "realized millennial" a better term?

Conclusion

Reformed and Presbyterian theology is Kingdom theology. We believe in the kingship or lordship of God and Christ. We see this lordship in different stages of redemptive history. God's lordship is evident in election and providence. His lordship is clear in our conversion. His kingship is clear in our Christian lives and in church and society. Our comfort lies in the fact that his kingship is also clear in the future.

As we look forward to the future coming of Christ, let us strive to make Christ king of our lives. Let us work for the establishing of his Kingdom in our world. Then we will be worthy to be accepted into his eternal kingdom. Then we will reign eternally with Christ.

Select Bibliography

1. Calvin's Writings: A Partial List

Calvin, John. *Calvin's New Testament Commentaries.* Edited by D.W. Torrance and T.F. Torrance. Grand Rapids: Wm. B. Eerdmans, 1963-1974.

Calvin, John. *Commentaries* [on the Old Testament]. 15 vols. Grand Rapids: Baker, 1979.

Calvin, John. *Institutes of the Christian Religion.* 2 vols. Edited by J.T. McNeill. Translated by F.L. Battles. Philadelphia: Westminster Press, 1960.

Calvin, John. *Institution of the Christian Religion* [1536 edition]. Translated by F.L. Battles. Atlanta: John Knox Press, 1975.

Calvin, John. *Letters of John Calvin.* 4 vols. Edited by J. Bonnet. Translated by D. Constable and M.R. Gilchrist. Grand Rapids: Baker, 1983

Calvin, John. *Letters of John Calvin Selected from the Bonnet Edition.* Edinburgh: The Banner of Truth Trust, 1980.

Calvin, John. *Tracts and Treatises.* 3 vols. Translated by H. Beveridge. Grand Rapids: Baker, 1983.

The Register of the Company of Pastors of Geneva in the Time of Calvin. Edited and translated by Philip E. Hughes. Grand Rapids: Wm. B. Eerdmans, 1966.

2. General Sources

Berkhof, Louis. *Systematic Theology.* Edinburgh: The Banner of Truth Trust, 1939.

Boer, Jan H. *Missions: Heralds of Capitalism or Christ?* Ibadan: Daystar Press, 1984.

De Witt, John R. *What is the Reformed Faith?* Edinburgh: The Banner of Truth Trust, 1981.

Kuyper, Abraham. *Lectures on Calvinism.* Grand Rapids: Wm. B. Eerdmans, 1931.

Kuyper, Abraham. *Souvereiniteit in eigen Kring.* Kampen: Kok, 1930.

McNeill, John T. *The History and Character of Calvinism.* Oxford: Oxford University Press, 1954.

Meeter, Henry H. *The Basic Ideas of Calvinism.* Revised by Paul Marshall. 6th edition. Grand Rapids: Baker, 1990.

Palmer, Edwin H. *The Five Points of Calvinism.* Grand Rapids: Baker, 1972.

Palmer, Timothy P. "John Calvin's View of the Kingdom of God." Ph.D. dissertation, University of Aberdeen, 1988.

Reid, W. Stanford, ed. *John Calvin: His Influence in the Western World.* Grand Rapids: Zondervan, 1982.

Spykman, Gordon. *Reformational Theology: A New Paradigm for Doing Dogmatics.* Grand Rapids: Wm. B. Eerdmans, 1992.

Walker, Williston. *A History of the Christian Church.* 3rd ed. New York: Charles Scribner, 1970.

Wendel, Francois. *Calvin: The Origins and Development of his Religious Thought.* Translated by Philip Mairet. London: Collins, 1965.

Wolters, Albert M. *Creation Regained: A Transforming View of the World.* Grand Rapids: Wm. B. Eerdmans, 1985.

3. Sources on Nigeria

Ahmadu, Ibrahim Musa. "Ekan Takum Schism: The Kuteb Narratives." B.A. Thesis, University of Jos, 1979.

Ajayi, J.F.A. *Christian Missions in Nigeria 1841-1891: The Making of a New Elite.* London: Longmans, 1965.

Ayandele, E.A. *Missionary Impact on Modern Nigeria 1842-1914: A Political and Social Analysis.* London: Longmans, 1966.

Beets, Henry. *Johanna of Nigeria.* Grand Rapids: Grand Rapids Printing Co., 1937.

Boer, Jan. *Missionary Messengers of Liberation in a Colonial Context: A Case Study of the Sudan United Mission.* Amsterdam: Rodopi, 1979.

Casaleggio, E.N. *Die Land Sal Sy Vrug Gee.* Elsierivier: N.G. Kerk, 1965.

Corbett, Jean S. *According to Plan: The Story of Samuel Alexander Bill, Founder of the Qua Iboe Mission, Nigeria.* Belfast: Qua Iboe Fellowship, 1977.

Crampton, E.P.T. *Christianity in Northern Nigeria.* London: Geoffrey Chapman, 1975.

Dokong, Alisabatu N.K. *Tarihin Zumunta Mata ERCC 1942-1992.* Akwanga: ERCC, 1992.

Ferguson, John. *Some Nigerian Church Founders.* Ibadan: Daystar, 1971.

Groves, C.P. *The Planting of Christianity in Africa.* Vol. 1. London: Lutterworth Press, 1944.

Hildebrandt, Jonathan. *The History of the Church in Africa.* Achimota: Africa Christian Press, 1981.

Livingstone, W.P. *Mary Slessor of Calabar: Pioneer Missionary.* London: Hodder & Stoughton, 1915.

McFarlan, Donald M. *Calabar: The Church of Scotland Mission 1846-1946.* London: Thomas Nelson, 1946.

Manga, Michael. *Tarihin Evangelical Reformed Church of Christ (ERCC) 1916-1991.* Akwanga: ERCC, 1991.

Maxwell, J. Lowry. *Half A Century of Grace.* London: Sudan United Mission, [1954].

Nigeria Reformed Church. *Constitution.* [1987.]

Qua Iboe Church. *Manual of Doctrine and Practice.* Etinan: Q.I.C. Printing Press, n.d.

RECON. *The Constitution of the Reformed Ecumenical Council of Nigeria.* 1992.

Rubingh, Eugene. *Sons of Tiv.* Grand Rapids: Baker, 1969.

Sanneh, Lamin. *West African Christianity: The Religious Impact.* Maryknoll, N.Y.: Orbis, 1983.

Smith, Edgar H. *Nigerian Harvest.* Grand Rapids: Baker, 1972.

Smith, Edgar. *TEKAS: Fellowship of Churches.* Jos: TEKAS Literature Committee, 1969.

Veenstra, Johanna. *Pioneering for Christ in the Sudan.* Grand Rapids: Smitter Book Co., 1926.